Getting to the Other Side of Emotional Pain

Dr. Ronnie Moore, Esq.

GETTING TO THE OTHER SIDE OF EMOTIONAL PAIN

Copyright © 2012 by Dr. Ronnie Moore, Esq.
Published by Blessed Capri Publishing
A Division of Choosing Hope Ministries, Inc.
DBA/ Blessed Capri Publishing, 9035 Baltimore Street
Savage, MD 20763
All rights reserved, this book is protected by the copyright laws of the United States of America. This book may not be copied or reprinted for commercial gain or profit. The use of short quotations or occasional page copying for personal or group study is permitted and encouraged. Permission will be granted upon request. Unless otherwise identified, Scripture quotations are taken from the New King James Version. Copyright 1982 Thomas Nelson, Inc. Used by permission. All rights reserved. Scripture quotations marked KJV are taken from The Holy Bible, King James Version
Blessed Capri Publishing, 9035 Baltimore Street, Savage, MD 20763.
For information regarding special discounts for purchases made in bulk, please contact Blessed-Capri Publishing at 1-855-382-4668 or visit our site at
www.blessedcapripublishing.org
ISBN 978-0-9858674-0-9
LCCN 2012915286
Printed in the United States of America

Dedication

First and foremost, I give thanks to the Almighty God for allowing me to share His love that has no boundaries in my life. I also thank Him for being first in my life. I know I made it because of your kindness, grace and mercy. I would also like to thank my grandparents, the late Rev. Ulysses Moore and Magnolia Davis Moore, who made sacrifices to allow me to further my education and taught me to keep Jesus as the head of my life. It is because of their great sacrifices that I am able to dedicate this work. I am very grateful to my father in the ministry, Dr. Claude T. Williams, who encouraged me to obtain as much education as I could. I thank God for Mrs. Marsha Clark/Moore, for the relentless hours of typing, research, editing, and proofing. My prayer is that God bestow a double anointing on each individual that contributed to work of God. I thank God for Ms. Sheila SmithAnthony for all of her prayers and support through the journey. I thank God for Mrs. Beverly Brown who prayed relentlessly through this journey. I thank God for my class leader, Mrs. Alfreida Witherspoon, you will forever be my class leader, Thank you God for the Virtuous women you placed in my life.

Acknowledgement

I would like to thank Bishop Richard Arno for his guidance in this journey. When I think of Bishop Arno, decent and in order would be my description. A man of integrity and a word of God, he is. Dr. Phyllis Arno. One word would be who she is, **virtuous!**

I give thanks for Bishop Adul Rasheed for his leadership in my life. A man of God's own hearth and integrity. Thank you for your guidance and being the example of Jesus Christ in your ministry. The encouragement you gave. The love you shared! The home you open up! It was truly a bridge from God. May God continue to shower you and your wife with his presents, love and abundants.

I like to thank Dr. Willie Mason for allowing me to share my gift with his congregation; it is because of opportunities like this which continue to fuel the work of the Lord, God Almighty. A true man of God with the proclivities to speak a word and you feel it in your heart. God bless you.

I Thank Elder Leroy Parker for his prayers! I thank him for his Godly advice, along with his encouragement when called upon. To provide an ear to listen and wait on God he would say to provide you the wisdom you need to move forward.

Table of Contents

CHAPTER ONE INTRODUCTION..................................9

Statement of the Problem......................................12

Statement of Limitation..15

Biblical/Theological Basis.....................................16

Statement of Methodology...................................19

Review of Literature...24

CHAPTER TWO: CREATION THERAPY..............39

What is Temperament...41

How to Counsel Each Temperament....................51

Temperament and Birth Order............................56

CHAPTER THREE A BASIC UNDERSTANDING OF PAIN..58

Emotional Pain..76

Worshipping Through Pain...............................80

Prayer Brings Change..84

CHAPTER FOUR: PREPARATIONS FOR GETTING PAST THE PAIN...95

Make Jesus Your Best Friend an Rock............,...............95

Daily Bible Reading..102

Pray to God Every Day....................................106

Share Your Beliefs With Like-minded People..........116

Keep Your Heart Pure......................................119

Let Jesus Avenge..121

Let Jesus Be Your Peace of Mind......................124

CHAPTER FIVE:RESEARCH/CASESTUDY..........133

The Law School..137

Foreclosure I...141

Foreclosure II..143

Bench Warrant..145

Worker's Compensation...147

Case Studies..152

Summary..194

CONCLUSION..195

How to Deal with Pain..195

God Can Change Anything Through Prayer.........201

Steps in Moving Past Pain..205

God's Make Over...217

Accept Christ's Invitation...222

BIBLIOGRAPY..226

DISCLAIMER

This book is designed to provide information on Getting to the Other Side of Emotional Pain. It is sold with the understanding that the publisher and author are not engaged in rendering legal, accounting or other professional services. If legal, clinical or other expert assistance is required, please contact: chmclacc.org or bcp@gmail.com.

Every effort has been made to make this manual as complete and accurate as possible. The purpose of this manual is to educate and inform. The author and Blessed Capri Publishing have neither liability nor responsibility to any person or entity with respect to any loss or damage caused, or alleged to have been caused, directly or indirectly, by the information contained in this book

For a more professional guide, appointment or consultation, contact: Rev. Dr. Ronnie Moore, MBA., Esq. at chmclacc@gmail.com or firstlaw1@gmail.com.

Chapter One

The purpose of this book, a previously submitted thesis, is to inform, instruct, educate and explore methods of how to deal with emotional pain. At Choosing Hope Ministries Christian Legal Aid & Clinical Counseling (CHMCLACC), there are a myriad of programs offered to help people to overcome painful situations. Dealing with emotional pain can be a bit confusing because in order to overcome and move on, one must first find the root of their problem. At CHMCLACC, clients are taught through a series of interviews, counseling sessions, group meetings, etc. how to recognize the state of their emotions and how to take the necessary steps to get to the other side.

At CHMCLACC, there are a few models that have been used when helping clients to deal with painful issues. One of the models in place is using the APS Report. This report will give the counselor a better understanding of the individual and their temperament. Another aspect of this model is it teaches one to embrace a deeper understanding of their personality, which in turn, assists in dealing with hurtful experiences.

The book will be precise. First, this book will not deal with physical pain. It will address emotional, spiritual and mental pain. It will not address questions of how to move past physical pain such as what you should take, who would be the best person to see, or how this physical pain will affect the body. This study will not deal with all areas of hurt and pain. This project will not include those who choose not to operate under God's power in their lives. The project's research will focus on helping Christians identify their hurt, deal with the hurt and move to the other side of their pain. It will provide the tools to identify their temperament. This is very important because it will make a difference in how one will respond. I will touch on the understanding of pain as well as the emotional components, the steps used to move to the other side. Lastly, the book will be limited to the hurt and pain of the mind. In order to be successful, one must be willing to express openly and honestly about the root of the pain and apply the correct approach to address the pain. At times, it may seem as if the weight of suffering and sorrow will conquer everyone. People hurt, families hurt, friendships hurt, relationships and marriages hurt, churches hurt, communities hurt and above all, entire nations hurt. What can be done about all of this pain and suffering? This will not be accomplished from sheer strength of will. The reason to trust God is that God chooses not to stand apart from our suffering. God has never been nor will He ever not be moved by the pain that His children suffer. He will embrace that pain and suffering right along with His children. God would rather be unblessed with His creatures than to be a blessed God of unblessed creatures. Jesus too, walked to the place of sacrifice, carting on his own back, the wood on which he was to be put to death. Just like Abraham, Jesus had to walk the road of "God-forsakenness," as he cried out, "My God, My God, why have you forsaken me?" (Matthew 27:46 NKJV). When Jesus was bound, no voice cried out to stay the ropes. When the blade pierced his body, no power held it back. This time, no other sacrifice was provided. This time, the Son died and the Father grieved. But then, the third came, as it will come someday for all. In the meantime, don't give up. First, let's thank God for those painful times because if those situations will make people seek Him out, it can only be a benefit to them. In order to achieve success in overcoming pain, one must also repent. Repent in a way that will mean something and make a difference. There are many things to do in order to move past uncomfortable situations. Just like a garden, one must prune away the weeds, thorns, sticks, etc., anything that needs to be done, get it done. By cooperating with God, things and situations can only get better with each step. Change may not come overnight, but change is sure to come. God is a great physician, and it is good to be pruned and drained. People ought to do it more often. For without surgery, margin and health will not return. Also, let's cooperate with God. The only hope for the future is only valid because of one fact: God is still around and even more important, He's still interested. The success and failures of everyone will hinge on their cooperation with God. "When this little life is over, nearly all that makes the headlines in the newspapers or fills the bulletins on the radio will seem to be of purely temporary significance. But the work of those who have cooperated with God will remain, for it is part of His everlasting purpose."[1] Working through emotions will allow one to reach a wisdom that is more personal and more accurate than just the level of our intellect.

Statement of the Problem

Pain is known for its impact on one's life. It may be physical, mental or emotional. The devastation of pain will get one's full attention, regardless of the area of penetration. What is pain? According to Webster's Dictionary, it defines pain as a "symptom of some physical hurt or disorder; emotional distress, or an instance of unpleasant sensation." It also goes on to say that "pain is the condition of suffering, or anguish, especially mental, as opposed to pleasure." [2] The rationale for choosing this area of study will allow personal experiences to cause a breakthrough in someone's life. When pain has become so great that it has the full attention of its victim, and has taken all emotions from within, and has caused numbness, the findings and results can change and affect one's life greatly.

---

[1] J.B. Phillips, *For This Day;* ed. Denis Duncan (Waco, TX: Word, 1974). 180.

[2] Webster's Dictionary

The study of pain is a very valuable topic. The goal is to share the potential value of this topic and how the vehicle of pain will change your life completely. It will help you understand life and mature through the process of growing through pain's effects. The approach to this subject will describe what pain is. What impact does pain have on one's life? How can pain be dealt with? Why does pain have to be dealt with? When should one address the issues of pain? No matter what, every love relationship has little problems along the way that may be destructive.

How do we move through the process of pain? What will it take to move to the other side of pain? How do we apply the steps that will allow us to understand pain? Know that going through pain is a testimony of the powers of God, and realizing this is its healing process. What are some of the spiritual treatments for pain? How do we achieve the goals of comfort and dignity after the pain? How do we recognize the problems that we face when trying to move to the other side of pain? The book will be approached in real examples of people's lives. First, by helping each individual to be able to identify with their temperament and personality to better understand why people respond the way they do while in pain. This survey will approach the areas of pain – where it hurts. Surveys will be conducted and participants shall reach beyond the hurt. Pain will be identified and the steps to overcome that particular situation will be looked into. People experience a certain fear about pain; however, when you know where it is, what it is hurting, how much this hurt is affecting your life, this is when you realize that something must be done.

This book will help people to become survivors of any hurtful experiences they may have endured during the course of their lives. The project will also explore different steps one may take in order to achieve the ultimate goal of getting beyond their pain and moving on with their lives in a more positive and spiritual direction. One of the main topics this project will deal with will be emotional pain.

Emotional pain can be described as a heartache that results from a painful experience, such as the loss of a loved one. It can stem from depression, anxiety, disappointment, fear or guilt and it tends to worsen when you replay and relive painful or traumatic events that occurred in the past. Emotional pain can become crippling when your moods, relationships, personal and professional, are affected and occupies your mind constantly.

What causes emotional pain: Many people experience emotional trauma during their childhood from a variety of factors, such as neglect, abuse, abandonment, or loss of a parent. Emotional pain during adulthood may occur from the end of a relationship, divorce, loss of a loved one, being a victim of a crime, substance abuse, or loss of employment. Often, where severe trauma is experienced, the person may be continuously haunted by recurring nightmares and mental images, as in the case of a war veteran or rape victim. Others who suffer from emotional pain may find themselves unable to stop dwelling on past hurts and disappointments and may struggle to let go of their painful memories. They may find themselves in a cycle of guilt and punishment, reliving the event over and over again in their minds.

As a result, individuals may fall into depression. They may find themselves plagued with feelings of worthlessness or hopelessness. Some hide their pain or avoid facing their emotional trauma by resorting to self-destructive behavior, such as alcohol or drug abuse, aggression, repression, or denial. Although it may seem like a coping mechanism, these actions are usually a cry for help. At one point, one must take a look at the entire situation and work hard to begin the process of overcoming their situations. One must realize that not all threshold limits are appreciated as we get closer to them, but it is only in exceeding them that we suddenly feel the break down.

Statement of Limitations

This book will discuss, first of all, to the type of pain that will be dealt with will not be physical pain. Questions of how to move past physical pain will not be addressed. Physical areas of pain and hurt will be omitted in this book. The results of this book will only include persons who choose to operate under God's laws and instructions. This project will focus on identifying varying ways in dealing with hurtful situations and moving to the other side of pain. Lastly, this study will be limited to the emotional pain; pain that has the power to destroy or ruin one's life. It will also be limited to the willingness to express openly and honestly the root of the pain and apply the correct approach to address the pain that one feels inside.

BIBLICAL/THEOLOGICAL BASIS
Job

"Man is also chastened with pain on his bed; And with strong pain in many of his bones." Job 33:19 (NKJV).

God sends afflictions for good. Job complained of his diseases, and he judged by them that God was angry with him. This is very common among someone who is experiencing a painful situation. Job's friends also thought so, but Elihu shows that God often afflicts the body for the good of the soul. This thought will be a great use for our recovering from sickness. God speaks to men. Pain is the fruit of sin. Yet, by the grace of God, the pain of the body is often made as a means of good to the soul. When afflictions have done their work, it shall be removed. A ransom or propitiation is found. Jesus Christ is the messenger and the ransom, so Elihu calls him, as Job had called him his Redeemer. Many times, one may think that God is punishing them for a sin done; and oftentimes, the question is asked: "Why Me?" Well, after much thought, instead of asking that question, should one ask: "Why Not Me?" When one realizes what Job had to endure, what Jesus gave up, the answer to that question should be a simple, "Thank you God." Without God's grace and mercy, one may never survive a painful situation. When one truly repents of their sins, they shall find true mercy with God. "If we confess our sins, He is faithful and just to forgive us our sins and to cleanse us from all unrighteousness." 1 John 1:9 (NKJV).

Revelation

"Then the fifth angel poured out his bowl on the throne of the beast, and his kingdom became full of darkness; and they gnawed their tongues because of the pain." Revelation 16:10 (NKJV)

Sometimes people are ignorant of the history of human nature, of the Bible and of their own hearts. People may not know that the more a man may suffer, and the more plainly they see the hand of God in their sufferings, the more they often rage against Him. Opposed to darkness and wisdom is darkness. It is opposed to pleasure and joy and signifies anguish and vexation of the spirit.

Genesis

"Because you have heeded the voice of your wife, and have eaten from the tree of which I commanded you, saying, 'You shall not eat of it: Cursed is the ground for your sake; in toil you shall eat of it, All the days of your life." Genesis 3:17 (NKJV)

The above scripture describes the pain and suffering that Adam and Eve would suffer from disobeying the Word of God. When one deliberately goes against God's instructions, they are at risk of dealing with not so pleasant consequences. Not realizing the magnitude of his actions, Adam listened to Eve and partook of the forbidden tree, the Lord was grieved that He had made man on earth, and His heart was filled with pain.

Against God's command, Adam and Eve made a bad choice by eating from the tree of the knowledge of good and evil. It was instantly that they knew they had done something wrong. In their disgrace, they tried their best to hide from God. It is because of these actions that led to calamity for all humankind, and to this day, we reap those terrible, and sometimes, painful consequences.

Statement of Methodology

The book will show when using the Arno Profile System, which is designed to get to the root of the problem will provide valuable information to CHMCLACC Model. The information will provide steps, when one is dealing with pain that they feel they can't get through. It will also reveal that the understanding of pain and the components that make up the hurt. When following a process or Worshipping through the pain, begin to pray for God's Mercy and Grace so we can move forward. The information will show that if we make Jesus our best friend, read the bible daily, pray to God daily, and fellowship with those who share our same beliefs, keep our hearts pure, let Jesus avenge and allow Jesus to be your peace of mind, then, we can move through the process of pain. Finally the research will identify the issue and provide steps to deal with moving to the other side of the pain. This book will offer a myriad of steps, examples, and tools to assist and guide someone to move past painful experiences and begin a new life in happiness. Many times people feel that they are all alone, and there is no help for them. However, the information will instruct individuals on how to identify their problems, accept what is happening, and, eventually, overcome their pain.

In Chapter One, we will address the issues dealing with emotional, spiritual, and mental pain. The information will focus on identifying the hurt, dealing with the hurt and moving to the other side of pain. Information will be limited to the hurt and pain of the mind and the cross. However, if the pain you feel can be identified as the pain on the cross, you have a way to healing. It will also be limited to the willingness to express openly and honestly the root of the pain and apply the correct approach to address the pain Chapter Two takes a look at Creation Therapy and the five temperaments used to identify the individual types. This test is based on the APS Model, founded by Richard and Phyllis Arno. This chapter will show the differences in the five personality types as described by the Arnos' in "Creation Therapy" (1) Sanguine: The Sanguine temperament personality is fairly extroverted. People of a sanguine temperament tend to enjoy social gatherings, making new friends and tend to be quite loud. They are usually quite creative and often daydream. They are talkative and not shy; (2) Choleric: A person who is choleric is a doer. They have a lot of energy, passion and ambition which they try to instill in others. People with this temperament can dominate people of other temperaments, especially phlegmatic types. They also tend to be leaders; (3) Melancholic: The melancholic is someone who is a thoughtful ponderer and has a melancholic disposition. Often very considerate and get rather worried when they could not be on time for events, people whom are melancholic can be highly creative in activities such as arts and poetry and can become occupied with the tragedies in the world. They are also often a perfectionist. They are often self-reliant and independent; one negative part of being a melancholic is sometimes they can get so involved in what they are doing they forget to think of others; (4) Phlegmatic: People who exhibit this characteristic tend to be self-content and kind. They can be very accepting and affectionate. They may be very receptive and shy and often prefer stability to uncertainty and change. They are very consistent, relaxed, rational, curious, and observant, making them good administrators. However, they can also be very passive aggressive; and (5) Supine: The dictionary definition of Supine is: "Lying on the back or with the face turned upward," "Having no interest or care, inactive." However, Supine's do have many interests, but they do not express them. They are not inactive, but may be slow-paced.

Chapter Three, the understanding of pain is seen as a symptom. This chapter will show the various meanings of pain, such as psychological pain, which comes from suffering emotionally. It can be a very complex process in which the pain signal can be magnified. By recognizing the physical and emotional components, one can make a difference in how to manage pain. Spiritual pain is a constant reminder of mortality. One will learn that the first step in controlling the pain is to understand what causes it. In dealing with emotional pain, one must realize that pain comes in a myriad of forms, be it the loss of a loved one, stress and anxiety, guilty anger, and so on.

Our course of action in emotional pain management involves two simple elements: awareness and planning. A simple example is to think of it this way: if you permit yourself to be aware of a broken piece of glass, you will not step on it with your bare foot. Another step that will be used in controlling pain is to understand the two components of pain. However, there is also acute and chronic pain. When dealing with emotion pain, culture and family play an important role in helping to form beliefs as how one "should" experience pain. Also personality and temperament can greatly affect the physiological process in which the brain sends electrical and chemical signals to open or close the pain gates.

In Chapter Four, one shall see that preparing to get over the pain can be easier than they may expect. The first thing to learn is to give their pain over to God. Normally, one will reach out to family and friends when they are going through trials and tribulations. In this chapter, one will learn how they can make Jesus their friend. By simply surrendering to Him, and allowing Him to guide them, half of the battle is over.

By taking the same amount of time spent complaining about our painful situations, one must learn to use that time to pray. The more time spent praying, the less time spent focusing on their problems. The list of steps used by Choosing Hope Ministries has helped their clients to better deal with the tribulations they have experienced in the past, and they now have the knowledge of how to handle and work through these situations in the future.

In Chapter Five, the first thing one must learn is the anatomy of pain. According to Anatomy of Pain, "Pain is a perception, not really a sensation, in the same way that vision and hearing are. It involves sensitivity to chemical changes in the tissues and then interpretation that such changes are harmful. This perception is real, whether or not harm has occurred or is occurring. Cognition is involved in the formulation of this perception. There are emotional consequences and behavioral responses to the cognitive and emotional aspects of pain. "Pain is a complex perception that takes place only at higher levels of the central nervous system."

The book will take an in depth look to see which of the participants had the desire to follow the model used by CHMCLACC, in order to overcome their painful situations. It will consist of the ability or potential to think outside of the box. The survey will also distinguish if a person is locked in a traditional mode and very closed minded. However; the areas that were addressed have a very important role in one's day to day life. The outcome of this evaluation revealed that 85% of the participants answered "True" to eighty-five percent or more of the evaluation questions. The evaluation also showed that those 85% were active members in their churches.

However; the 15% of the participants answered "True" to less than 15% of the questions. This same 15% also revealed that they were not active in any organized religion and were not successful in overcoming their situations. One of the main reasons for this is they did not agree that using the Bible and scriptures would be a major factor in assisting them to overcome these situations. This evaluation also revealed that the participants in the 15% group had a greater number of "False" answers in this questionnaire; which would indicate an earlier realization regarding the ability to follow the model used to make the necessary, life-altering changes and succeed.

REVIEW OF LITERATURE

This review of the literature is designed to provide resources that can assist in a better understanding of how to overcome painful situations and steps that may aid in a successful transformation. Richard and Phyllis Arnos conducted research to develop a scripturally-based therapeutic system that would give them an effective and positive result in dealing with those in need of counseling or guidance, or "Creation Therapy."

The Arnos' research was based on 5,000 participants, who sought counseling for marriage and dysfunctional family situations, depression, anxiety and so on. The purpose of this research was to develop an accurate clinical testing procedure for initial identification of the counselee's inborn, God-given tendencies and temperaments. In-depth studies were conducted, during this same time, on all of the current psychological tests and/or behavioral inventories. The Arnos selected the FIRO-B, which was developed by Will Schultz, as their initial measure device or questionnaire. The Arnos named their analysis procedure the Temperament Analysis Profile (T.A.P.) and subsequently changed it in November 2000 to the Arno Profile System. This system reveals the hidden problems that normally take the counselor seven or eight sessions to identify. Currently, the Arno Profile System is being used by over 3,000 Christian leaders, ministers and professional Christians to aid them in their counseling efforts. These Christians report an "accuracy rate of over 90 percent in identifying an individual's inborn, God-given temperament."[3]

In T.D. Jakes' *Maximize the Moment*, he teaches us that we don't have to settle for less as well as teaches how to face the many obstacles that may hinder our growth. This book shows us how to get from under difficult situations and move toward a better life by using our God-given talents.

---

[3] Richard Gene Arno and Phyllis Jean Arno, Creation Therapy: A Biblically Based Model for Christian Counseling (Sarasota Academy of Christian Psychology, 1993). 49.

Self Matters by Dr. Phil McGraw touches on working on your "authentic" self by taking a good look at yourself and addressing any issue from the inside out. This book shows us how a person should look at the facts when taking a look at their lives and to overcome the things that are hindering us from living the lives that we've always wanted.

The Apostle Paul wrote the same thing: "Forgetting those things which are behind, reaching forth unto those things which were before. I press toward the mark of my higher calling."

Self-realization and self-awareness are vital to our lives. Because of the way a person thinks results in him feeling the way he does. If you are feeling down and out, nearly every thought that comes into your mind will be a negative thought. More times than not, when you are at your lowest in life, you start viewing others in the worse possible way. Not that you are hopeless, you do tend to feel you're in a state of hopelessness. Do not make the mistake that your feelings are your reality.

Get positive encouragement from others. Make it a point to be around people who make you feel good about yourself, whether friends, family, coworkers, or mentors such as teachers and coaches. "Commit right now to requiring more of yourself, for yourself in every area of your life."[4] It is understandable that one may not know exactly how to do this but if you just take the time to make a commitment to make the necessary changes, it will make adjusting to overcoming painful situation a little easier. However, it is hard to stay committed to something that may seem difficult, but if the client is serious about turning his life around, this is an important step he must be willing to take.

Give yourself internal encouragement. Concentrate on saying things and doing volunteer work, working out, taking a class, listening to music or motivational tapes. Reading inspirational books and the Bible, anything that makes you feel good about you. Get in the habit of saying positive things to you. Find a positive expression or several that work for you and put them on a card where you can look at them during the day. Lastly, he states: "I have to break the spell, and talk about what I am going through. I have to talk about the shame and the fear. Our purpose as survivors is to not lose ourselves in the feelings of emotional bankruptcy, chaos and pain that come with the loss. We have to learn how to combat the genetic paths, the depressions and the sometimes preordained feelings that we, too, must follow that devastating path.

---

[4] Phillip C. McGraw. *Life Strategies: Doing What Works, Doing What Matters*. NY. Hyperion, 1999. 288.

World War Me, by Pastor Jamal-Harrison Bryant, is the straightforward and repentant approach of self-reflection of a man who finds himself broken. Bryant uses his personal experiences of heartbreak, brokenness, and the consequences from wrong decisions, which cost him his integrity and defeat to show us how to overcome self-defeat. This book is an instructional guide in overcoming attacks by the enemy — whether it is temptation, fear, desperation, and so on, and provides solutions to winning the war."

In Greg Schmitt's article *What Is Emotional Pain and What Does It Tell Us?*, he states that pain is something we all have experienced thousands of times throughout our lifetime. We have been in a situation that is out of our comfort zone, and once this happens we run from the fear because we have entered a situation of the unknown. Then massive negative thoughts settle in our minds leaving us in a depressed state. This is apparent when someone starts the "greatest home business opportunity" hoping for that instant financial turnaround. They jump into an opportunity without knowing the disciplines and skills that are necessary for success. Emotional pain sets in, leading to frustration and misery because of this new adventure and momentarily getting out of their comfort zone.

In *Further Along the Road Less Traveled*, by M. Scott Peck, we learn that "more importantly, the most healing thing that we can do with someone who is in pain, rather than trying to get rid of that pain, is to be there and be willing to share it. We have to learn to hear as well as bear other people's pain. That is all a part of becoming more conscious. As we grow spiritually, we can take on more and more of other people's pain. The more pain you are willing to take on, the more joy you will also begin to feel. This makes the journey worthwhile."[5]

While reading Richard Carlson's *Easier Than You Think Because Life Doesn't Have to be So Hard* we learn that when dealing with pain, hope is one of the most powerful forces in our lives."[6] Hope keeps us happy instead of depressed, giving us something to look forward to in our future instead of dwelling in the past. Regardless of our circumstances, knowing there's a chance that we can overcome this pain makes a huge difference. Hope is one thing that keeps the human spirit alive. It gives us reason to go on, even when we're going through rough times."

---

[5] Peck, Scott. *Further Along the Road Less Traveled: The Unending Journey* Toward Spiritual Growth (New York: Touchstone, 1993), 21–24.

[6] Carlson, Richard. *Easier Than You Think Because Life Doesn't Have to be So Hard* (New York: Harpers Collins, 2005), 23, 38, 40, 43.

The Depression Cure by Stephen Ilardi shows how a person can overcome depression without the use of traditional drugs. His use of Therapeutic Lifestyle Change program has proven to be quite effective in helping people to overcome depression. He introduces a 6-step program for beating depression.

In Desmond Tutu's *God Has a Dream,* he offers a personal view of how suffering can be turned into something great. After spending 27 years locked in a South African prison, Mr. Tutu used those desperate times to build up the strength and courage to overcome his dire situation. This book was written to encourage the millions of South Africans who are still struggling for basic human rights. More importantly, he reaches out to people of all faiths and religions to show them how they too can reach a point of redemption.

T.D. Jakes' *Naked and Not Ashamed* shows how those who are believers, need to take away all of their layers, in order to get to the root of their issues. Many times, folks will hide behind certain issues in order to avoid what's really going on in their lives. Bishop Jakes wants us to be real just as Jesus died in openness for the sins of the world.

In Larry Crabb's book *Connecting: Healing for Ourselves and Our Relationships* we learn that there are "three ingredients involved in the healing of ourselves as well as a community."[7]

First and foremost, we must surrender these feelings over to God. God assists us to become more like Christ by:

---

[7] Crabb, Larry. *Connecting: Healing for Ourselves and Our Relationships* (Nashville: W Publishing Group, 1997), 11.

(1) providing us a taste of Christ delighting in us—"connection"—accepting who we are and envisioning who we could be; (2) God searches within us for the good He has put there—"affirming exposure"—remaining calm when badness is visible and keeping confidence that goodness lies beneath; (3) God engagingly exposes what is bad and painful—"disruptive exposure"—claiming the special opportunities to reveal grace and that difficult content of our hearts provide.

Simply put, we may try everything in our power to deal with people and certain situations. But until we release and surrender to God, we will not get through. Instead of getting angry, allow the person to repent. Instead of dealing with the flesh and reacting off of our emotions, we should submit to the spirit of God.

Real Life Preparing for the 7 Most Challenging Days of Your Life, Dr. Phil McGraw helps in preparing you to confront what he believes is the seven critical days that you or someone you love may face. This book shows you how to be there for yourself when difficult days happen. This book will also show you how to make changes in your present life, before you get into a crisis as well as becoming a leader to someone during their crisis. Dr. Phil provides resources to help guide you to solutions to fit your problems by minimizing disruption and maximizing recovery.

Making Great Decisions: For a Life Without Limits, written by Bishop T. D. Jakes, CEO of TDJ Enterprises and founder and senior pastor of The Potter's House of Dallas. Bishop Jakes touches on the topic of relationships and guides you to the right track in order to make the decisions that will benefit you for your entire life. The five components mentioned are "(1) Research—gathering information and collecting data; (2) Roadwork—removing obstacles and clearing the paths; (3) Rewards—listing choices and imagining their consequences; (4) Revelation—narrowing your options and making your selection; and (5) Rearview—looking back and adjusting as necessary to stay on course."[8]

The purpose *of Tried, Tested, and Triumphant: The Book of Job* by David Jeremiah, senior pastor of Shadow Mountain Community Church, is to reinforce in-depth teaching and to aid the reader in applying biblical truth to his or her daily life. The book takes us on a verse by verse guide of Job's challenging journey. Job released his grief to God by doing four things: "he arose, tore off his robe, shaved his head and fell to the ground; and by falling, Job worshipped, which angered Satan."[9]

---

[8] T. D. Jakes, *Making Great Decisions* (New York: Atria, 2008), 11.

[9] David Jeremiah, *Tried, Tested, and Triumphant: The Book of Job* (San Diego: Self-published, 2010), 17.

Singles Prepare! Before You Say I Do, by Frank and Joe Nell Summerfield, is written for people who are discouraged and disheartened, who may feel trapped in a mundane and average existence. The Summerfield' have spent more than thirty years proving the principles of marriage. One important piece of information is "you need to plan, not just a wedding, but also a marriage."[10]

Dr. Wayne Dyer's *Excuses Begone!*, points out how one learns how to change the old way of thinking and begin a new way in order to overcome fears and not make excuses of why we can't. This book teaches us how to identify when we are using a crutch or excuse in order to not move forward to be more productive and happier individuals.

Laura Schlessinger's *Surviving a Shark Attack (On Land)* takes a personal look at betrayal and revenge. She writes about her personal experience about how she felt after using the "N-word," on her radio show. She felt that if others have used it, and it's used by many in the music industry, it was okay. However, in today's society, she soon found out that this was not the case, and in turn, she felt betrayed from the backlash she received.

---

[10] Frank & Joe Nell Summerfield, *Singles Prepare! Before You Say I Do,"* (Chapel Hill, N: Amour of Light Publishing, 2009), 10.

Joshua Coleman's *When Parents Hurt* offers insight on how to have a successful relationship between a parent and child. He teaches how parents can learn to deal with their child's imperfections as well as their own. He has developed different strategies on rebuilding damaged relationships and how sometimes, the expectations of what society thinks a parent should be can be detrimental and contribute to a parent's self-doubt or downfall.

Living with Confidence in a Chaotic World, written by Dr. David Jeremiah, was written to show how the love and power of God, one can be confident even during a time of crisis. He uses the word of God for the answers that are plaguing the world today. This book will help you to find the courage, through the strength of Christ, to overcome uncertain times.

In *How to Turn Your Prison into Your Prosperity*, Frank Summerfield captures the concept of how all of us at one point in our lives become imprisoned in our minds by things or circumstances that had a major impact. Written with a scriptural base, it shows the reader how to turn their personal prisons, no matter how greatly affected and embedded in their minds, into their personal prosperity." Psychotherapist Mira Kirshenbaum's *Everything Happens for a Reason* will help us to understand the principles behind this frequently used phrase. It also provides us with tools to grasp its true meaning. Kirshenbaum has developed tests to help readers decode the confusing or unfortunate events in their lives and find peace and strength in the positive outcomes. Kirshenbaum offers ten universal reasons for the tragedies in our lives.

Victoria Osteen's *Love Your Life, Living Happy, Healthy & Whole* deals how to take charge of your life and take control in how you live your life. Taking the necessary step and being able to see the "positive in every situation"[11]

Bishop T. D. Jakes' *Can You Stand to be Blessed?* Gives insight to help survive the peaks and valleys we all face. We learn in the Bible that we are to be renewed by the transforming of our minds. Only the Holy Spirit knows how to renew our minds. Our early opinion of ourselves is deeply affected by the opinions of authoritative people in our formative years. He talks about how a child's self-worth is damaged if they are ignored or neglected by their parent or care-giver. But once a person learns they do not need to be validated by others, they will eventually be able to experience a new life.

The Great Investment by T.D. Jakes touches on the three things that are important to have a happier life: Faith, Family and Finance. This book demonstrates how Faith is the foundation of what one wants to achieve. Family keeps you grounded because it is the anchor and lastly, Finance equals success by helping us to get from one place to another.

---

[11] Victoria Osteen, *Love Your Life, Living Happy, Healthy & Whole* (New York: Free Press, 2008), 91.

In Vernon Whaley's *The Dynamics of Corporate Worship*, The purpose of corporate worship is to engage God's people in expressing love, admiration, and exaltation of Jehovah God for who He is and for what He has done. It involves facilitating opportunities of praise and worship as one group, together. God promises to inhabit the praise of His people. Only as we bless, praise, adore, and magnify his holy name does God enable us to worship in power and truth.

Vernon Whaley's *Brokenness* is a prerequisite for genuine worship. We must be broken in spirit, broken of self, broken . . . and surrendered. The world certainly has done enough to break us. We live in a world of broken lives, broken marriages, broken homes, and broken hearts. But God is in the business of mending broken hearts, repairing relationships, and putting families back together, but before he can restore us to beauty, we must be broken before Him. We must come to him, with open hands, and surrender our wills as things unclean to a holy God. It is then, during our moment of total surrender, the He will reveal Himself at His best as Repairer, Restorer, and lover of our broken souls.

Pain surrounds us all. Much of this pain comes from progress's blatant disregard for our need of margin. And much of this pain—far too much of this pain—is because relational, emotional, and spiritual sickness is endemic. If you live in a swamp, malaria has a head start.

But do you know what? Malaria can be treated, and so can pain. Margin can be restored. Broken relationships can be healed. It takes work, it takes love. It might even take going to the cross, but healing is worth it all.

John Ortberg states: "The primary goal of spiritual life is human transformation."[12] But this takes time. Many times, clients want to rush and get to the other side. Without patience, this feat will be difficult because they, the client, must first understand what they are transforming from and transforming into.

---

[12] John Ortberg, *The Life You've Always Wanted* (Grand Rapids, MI: Zondervan, 2002). 21.

Give yourself internal encouragement. Concentrate on saying things and doing volunteer work, working out, taking a class, listening to music or motivational tapes. Reading inspirational books and the Bible, anything that makes you feel good about you. Get in the habit of saying positive things to yourself. Find a positive expression or several that work for you and put them on a card or post it note where you can view them during the day. Lastly, one must learn to break the spell and speak up about what they are going through. Do not fear talking about shame or fear. The purpose of survivors is to not lose themselves in the feelings of emotional bankruptcy, chaos or pain that may come with a loss. One has to learn how to combat the genetic paths and depressions and press on to move forward.

CHAPTER TWO

CREATION THERAPY

One of the models used at Choosing Hope Ministries Christian Legal Aid & Clinical Counseling Center (to be referred throughout as CHMCLACC) in assisting clients and counselees in overcoming traumatic and painful situations is Creation Therapy. Creation Therapy is based on a program started by Dr's Richard and Phyllis Arno. Creation Therapy is based on the use of temperaments and uses the outcome of the study to help in understanding one's inner self. Although this concept is fairly new, it has been deemed very successful. Creation Therapy is used to identify the temperament needs in the clients and assists them in finding a balance in order to relieve and reduce inner stress and conflict.

Creation Therapy, is based using the "theory of temperament (which is the understanding of the inner man)"[13] according to Drs. Arno, who go on to say that it is not the "perfect solution for all of man's problems,"[14] but it allows the counselee to get a better understanding of who they are and how their minds work.

---

[13] Richard & Phyllis Arno. *Creation Therapy: A Biblically Based Model for Christian Counseling.* (2003). vi

[14] ____. Ibid., vi

According to Drs. Arno, the "counseling was solely the responsibility of the church during the early establishment of Christianity."[15] CHMCLACC takes a more in depth and innovated approach in how they counsel those in need. Along with using Creation Therapy as a guide, CHMCLACC has also implemented counseling in business and legal areas as well by addressing painful and emotional situations that may accompany these issues. For instance, a client comes in and is emotionally distressed and hurt due to a foreclosure, bankruptcy or any legal issues. Most counselors will only address the emotional pain of loss the client may be experiencing. However, at CHMCLACC, clients are taught the structure of how foreclosures, bankruptcies, etc. are done. Clients are educated in the laws, rules and regulations of the issues they are dealing with instead of how the situation has affected them emotionally.

Simply put, according to Drs. Richard and Phyllis Arno, "therapeutic methods that were developed by the secular community, such as Reality Therapy by Glasser or Client-Centered Therapy by Carl Rogers, were applied using a biblical approach."[16]

---

[15] ____. Ibid., v

[16] Ibid., v

One very important subject that is learned from Drs. Arno is that Creation Therapy "must be used for good."[17] The reason for this is there is a law that states what is discussed between a counselee and counselor is privileged information and should be kept confidential. Imagine the devastation that a counselor can cause a counselee by sharing this information with the wrong person or company. The counselee would be at risk of being hurt, humiliated, or even black mailed if their personal information was received by the wrong person.

Lastly, Creation Therapy, according to Drs. Arno, is a very "successful therapeutic process because it teaches us to take a 'look at the fruit,' and this is evidence that it is of God and has His anointing."[18]

What is Temperament?

Temperament is defined as the part of a person that determines how they may react to places, things, people and situations. It is how people interact with their environment in which they live as well as everything around them. Temperament is also used in determining how well a person may or may not deal with situations that may be stressful or painful. In Creation Therapy, we learn that the "theory of temperament teaches that our temperament is placed within us by God, while in our mother's womb."[19]

---

[17] Ibid., vii

[18] Ibid. 19

[19] Ibid., vi

According to Tim LaHaye; the theory of the "four temperaments are not perfect, but it is the oldest on record, dating back over 3,000 years. In Proverbs 30:11-14, the wise man saw four kinds of people and it wasn't until five hundred years later that Hippocrates gave names to these temperaments. Around A.D. 200, Galen, a Greek doctor, provided a detailed list of the strengths and weaknesses of the four temperaments and has remained the same throughout history. However, according to Sigmund Freud's theories based human behavior on the background and environment rather than inherited."[20] In research done by Drs. Arno, they found that according to Paul D. Meier, et al, author of *Introduction to Psychology and Counseling, Christian Perspectives and Applications*, they all are in agreement that "character and behavior are correctable; physical defects seldom are."[21]

David Keirsey points out that "there is much more to be gained by appreciating the differences and to be lost by ignoring them, but the first step is to become better acquainted with your own traits of character and temperament."[22]

---

[20] Tim LaHaye. *Spirit Controlled Temperament.* (Illinois: Tyndale Publishers. 1994), 1.

[21] Richard Arno & Phyllis Arno, *Creation Therapy. A Biblically Based Model for Christian Counseling.* (2003). 1.

[22] David Keirsey *Please Understand Me II – Temperament, Character, Intelligence* (CA: Prometheus Nemesis Book Company, 1998), 4.

Any study regarding the temperaments should go back to Hippocrates, an early Greek doctor. Although there have been other studies regarding the temperaments, CHMCLACC follows the methods created by Drs. Arno and Tim LaHaye in their counseling center. According to Hippocrates, "man's behavior is governed by the color of bile within a person's body. These bodily fluids, which he called humors, were divided into four classifications: blood (sanguine), black bile (melancholic), yellow bile (choleric), and Phlegm (phlegmatic)."[23]

There are three elements of man, known as "Trichotomists," according to Creation Therapy. "The three elements are listed as: **The body** – physical part of man; **The soul** – simple understanding, emotion and sensibility; **The spirit** - the mind, principle of man's rational and immortal life."[24]

Let's take a look at the historical and scientific background of temperaments according the Drs. Arno. This is to give a brief history on just old the study of temperaments go.

Hippocrates (460-370 B.C.) – Hippocrates divided the temperaments into four separate categories: Blood (Sanguine), Black bile (Melancholy), Yellow Bile (Choleric) and Phlegm (Phlegmatic). These names were given because he associated a person's behavior to that fluid.

---

[23]Tim LaHaye. *Spirit Controlled Temperament.* (Illinois: Tyndale Publishers, 1994), vii.

[24] Richard Arno & Phyllis Arno, *Creation Therapy A Biblically Based Model for Christian Counseling.* (2003), 8.

CHMCLACC divides the temperaments to have a better understanding of the temperament that they are working with. It is understood that the temperament is very important where there is an attorney assigned to a client. It is believed that the beginning preparations that are made can and will have an effect on the working relationship. The fluid that Hippocrates spoke about will determine if the client is assertive or aggressive, quiet or direct, organized or dysfunctional. It will be determined if the process will move forward, hit a lump and sit still, fall down and choose to get up and deal directly head-on and precise.

The blood will determine if the client will act or react or be motivated at all times and refuse any feelings of defeat.

Galen (131-200) – Through physiological research, he sought for the reasons for the differing behavior in humans. Counselors at CHMCLACC agree with Galen that there is a difference in human behavior. It is more productive when we are able to understand that there are differences and those differences need to be addressed as such. By identifying these differences early will help to produce a more positive outcome. The clinic understands that each individual is unique and that is the beginning of getting to the root of the problem, which in turn, will help the client to get to the other of emotional pain.

Nicholas Culpeper (1616-1754) – Culpeper believed that there were only two temperaments, dominant (which would be a strong temperament) and recessive (a weak temperament). CHMCLACC also agrees that a client with a weaker temperament would require more as far as counseling as well as a better understanding of who them are. While meeting people at their needs, CHMCLACC believes that whether the temperament be strong or weak, once it is identified, an individual plan is then put together to address the clients personal situation.

Immanuel Kant (1724-1804) – Kant believed that temperaments were caused by the power and temperature of the blood. He also believed that a person can only have one temperament. CHMCLACC believes that when the process is complete, one temperament is mainly dealt with, even when two or three may exist. The most dominant temperament is the one that is addressed.

Alfred Adler (1879-1937) – Although he developed his own typo

logy of the four temperaments, he truly did not believe in them. He felt it was only useful in helping people learn of temperaments. At CHMCLACC, the belief is when a person knows who they are, or have the tools that will help identify who they are, they are more likely better prepared. The identity of an individual can be very shocking and overwhelming to the impact of how they will respond, digest, or process whatever circumstances they may find themselves in.

Ivan Pavlov (1849-1936) – Experienced in working with dogs, he also observed mental patients and concluded that because of the differences in the excitatory and inhibitory responses, he agreed with the temperaments of Hippocrates.

Hans J. Eysenck (1916-1997) – Eysenck's researched how to analyze differences in personalities using a psychostatistical method, leading him to believe temperament is biologically based. CHMCLACC accepts this belief in the area of human make up. The belief is (Yellow Bile) will be controlling and direct in its action whereas (Black Bile) Melancholy will be a more reasonable responding person.

Tim LaHaye (1926-) – LaHaye is the author of over twenty books, and four of these books are on the topic of temperaments and hot it relates to human behavior.

This history reported by Richard and Phyllis Arno was shown to support that there is a "strong scientific and historical base for the study of temperament."[25]

The following descriptions were taken from Drs. Arnos' book Creation Therapy.

---

[25] Ibid., 21FF

"Sanguine: The Sanguine temperament personality is fairly extroverted. People of a sanguine temperament tend to enjoy social gatherings, making new friends and tend to be quite loud. They are usually quite creative and often daydream. However, some alone time is crucial for those of this temperament. Sanguine can also mean very sensitive, compassionate and thoughtful. Sanguine personalities generally struggle with following tasks all the way through, are chronically late, and tend to be forgetful and sometimes a little sarcastic. Often, when pursuing a new hobby, interest is lost quickly when it ceases to be engaging or fun. They are very much people persons. They are talkative and not shy.

Choleric: A person who is choleric is a doer. They have a lot of energy, passion and ambition which they try to instill in others. People with this temperament can dominate people of other temperaments, especially phlegmatic types. They also tend to be leaders.

Melancholic: Is someone who is a thoughtful ponderer, has a *melancholic* disposition. Often very considerate and get rather worried when they could not be on time for events, people whom are melancholic can be highly creative in activities such as arts and poetry and can become occupied with the tragedies in the world. They are also often a perfectionist. They are often self-reliant and independent; one negative part of being a melancholic is sometimes they can get so involved in what they are doing they forget to think of others; and

Phlegmatic: People who exhibit this characteristic tend to be self-content and kind. They can be very accepting and affectionate. They may be very receptive and shy and often prefer stability to uncertainty and change. They are very consistent, relaxed, rational, curious, and observant, making them good administrators. However, they can also be very passive aggressive.

Supine: The dictionary definition of Supine is: "Lying on the back or with the face turned upward," "Having no interest or care, inactive." However, Supines do have many interests, but they do not express them. They are not inactive, but may be slow-paced."[26]

Tim LaHaye also goes on to say that "Temperament is the combination of inborn traits that subconsciously affect all our behavior. These traits, which are passed on by our genes, are based on hereditary factors and arranged at the time of conception. The alignment of temperament traits, though unseen, is just as predictable as the color of eyes, hair, or size of body."[27]

By using these standards, people are able to get a better and deeper understanding of him/her, which in turn, helps them to deal with any types of situations in their lives.

---

[26] Richard Arno and Phyllis Arno. *Creation Therapy. A Biblically Based Model for Christian Counseling.* (2003), 37ff.

[27] Tim LaHaye. *Spirit Controlled Temperament.* (Illinois: Tyndale Publishers, 1994), 2.

One reason the temperament is so important is it makes a person unique, and as counselors, we must offer counseling according to that uniqueness.

At CHMCLACC, counselors are trained to follow a series of steps during temperament counseling sessions developed by the Arnos. By following these steps, it has been found that clients were successful in overcoming their painful situations. This is a five step process beginning with the first counseling session.

In session one, the clients are given the Arno Profile System Response form. This form has a series of questions which helps the counselor identify a client's inborn temperament as well as providing the counselor with a clear understanding of the client and some of the things they may be experimenting. This session is very critical because at this point, the counselor does not know the client's temperament and may use the wrong approach and lose them from the very start. Counselors that have a full session on the first visit are apt to make serious mistakes.

Session two is when the client is asked by the counselor to share their feelings and any problems they may be going through. This session is where the counselor is the listener. It is important that the counselor take notes for future reference. Most of the things the counselee will reveal during this session will be dealing with overt problems such as "My spouse is having an affair," "I'm depressed," "I want a divorce."

It is also during this session that if it is found out that the counselee does not, or never had a personal relationship/experience with God, it is introduced. They are told about the plan of salvation. Counselors must realize that they just can't tell clients about salvation, they must also invite them to receive it.

In session three the client is taught about themselves and their unique needs. This also helps the counselor to understand why the client may be dealing with inner conflicts as well as conflict with others.

Session Four consists of examining each individual need of the client. By working together, the counselor will attempt to identify which needs are being met and the needs which aren't being met in a way which may be causing the client to experience painful situations or harm.

The last session is where the needs that have been unmet have been identified and the counselor and client will begin to determine which approach will be followed to meet these needs, and hopefully, in ways that will not cause any harm to the client, loved ones, or those around them.

How to Counsel Each Temperament

"To have a good perception and understanding the way the temperament's control of our actions and reactions, we should define three terms and carefully distinguish among them: temperament, character and personality."[28] When counseling a person with a Melancholy temperament, the initial approach is the most critical. The counselor must be gentle and use intellectual superiority. As the counselor, you must appear to be a person of authority and give them information and options so that they can make their own decisions. Most people with this temperament are rebels and will rebel against most kinds of pressure. No matter what, whatever they choose to do, it has to be their idea.

The counselor should never confront a Melancholy with their mistakes. It would be better to ask them if they think this was the right way to handle the situation than to tell them that they are wrong. By asking them if their problem can be handled in a different way gives them the opportunity to make that decision. One of the best things about counseling the Melancholy is that when they do decide to change, they change. However; it has to be their idea. One major point to remember when dealing with the Melancholy is due to their low self-esteem and poor self-image; they will mask this image with an air of superiority. They'll usually react in a strong-minded way and become controlling and impatient.

---

[28] Tim LaHaye. *Spirit Controlled Temperament.* Illinois: Tyndale Publishers. 1994. 3

Counseling the Choleric: Unlike the Melancholy, proving that you are intellectually superior will make them feel threatened. Cholerics normally have a high need for recognition. The best way to counsel a Choleric; is counseling in terms of how much more they will be blessed or receive by adjusting the patterns of their behavior. In a lot of instances, the Choleric's attitude is "I don't have a problem. The other person is the one with the problem."

Another important aspect of counseling a Choleric is to remember that you are dealing with someone who is goal-oriented and must gain something from the session. Cholerics are not the type who will seek counseling unless they know there is something in it for them. It is important not to show any type of doubt or weakness in your ability when counseling a Choleric.

Counseling the Sanguine: The important thing about counseling a Sanguine is that, because they are so optimistic, their situation normally has to deteriorate to the point where it is almost impossible before they will seek out counseling. Sanguines tend to be very genuine and will recognize the problem, and normally, will repent one day. However; if they are tempted the next day, they will go right back to the behavior that brought them to counsel in the first place. Set well-defined parameters and enforce them. This is difficult because getting a Sanguine to accept these parameters is nearly impossible. Normally, this could be accomplished by threats of punishment. However; the one thing that motivates the Sanguine is the promise of reward, the reward of acceptance, attention and approval.

The two key points that are important for the counselor to remember when counseling a Sanguine is first: the sessions should never go more than fifty minutes. This is because most Sanguines have a short attention span. By going over fifty minutes, the Sanguine will see this as a waste and will work against coming back for another session; and second: the Sanguine needs the counselor to be friendly. They communicate at deep levels of emotion.

Counseling the Supine: A person with the Supine temperament tends to be an extrovert who appears to be an introvert. They are relationship-oriented and the main reason they perform tasks is to make and retain their relationships. Being that they lose momentum and are slow-pace, a change in their environment will regenerate them. They are motivated by the fear of punishments. When counseling a Supine, the counselor must be willing to accept a degree of the Supine's dependency until that dependency can be transferred to God as well as the significant individual or individuals in their lives.

Supines have the need for emotional support as well as to receive recognition and to be taken care of. A counselor must never make decisions for the Supine. The counselor's responsibility is to teach them gradually how to make independent decisions and to accept the responsibility for them. The counselor must establish themselves as the ultimate authority. It is imperative to monitor their behavior. If it gets worse during counseling, they must not be rewarded by giving them more attention. Supines will take on any kind of behavior they deem appropriate in order to keep the attention of the counselor.

Counseling the Phlegmatic: Most Phlegmatics suffer from extremely low energy reserve, and by knowing this, it is a great help to the counselor. This low energy is a result of an inborn trait, so they have no control over it. Phlegmatics tend to be both extroverts and introverts, but they do not like to spend their energy on people. They are task-oriented and perform in order to make a living, not to establish relationships. They are motivated by a combination of intellect, promise of reward and fear of punishment. They are also complacent and pretty much happy with things the way they are.

It is important to be their friend. Show them that you understand and are going to work toward helping them have a more peaceful environment in which to live. The counselor should place a little responsibility on the counselee and not require them to do a lot of reading or homework. The counselor should not be overly energetic or enthusiastic. A slow, calm, peaceful approach will go further.

There are three areas of counseling according to Creation Therapy. They are "Inclusion, Control and Affection."[29]

Basic traits of Inclusion: extrovert of high intensity; relationship orientated; lives life at a very fast pace; motivated by the promise of reward and by the threat of punishment; very active; highly responsive to the five senses; optimistic and upbeat; fears rejection and very hot-tempered.

---

[29] Richard and Phyllis Arno, *Creation Therapy Creation Therapy A Biblically Based Model for Christian Counseling.* (2003), 37.

Basic traits of Control: independent/self-motivated; expresses very little control over lives and behaviors of others; makes decisions and takes on responsibility; good leadership capabilities; demands truth, order, reliability from self and others; must appear competent and in control; tends to be legalistic, uncompromising; uneasy or anxious if solely responsible for anyone, including self; will give advice when asked, but will not pressure them to follow this advice; becomes angry if confronted for mistakes, criticized or humiliated.

Basic traits of Affection: expresses and responds to a great deal of love and affection; needs to establish and maintain deep personal relationships with many people; communicated by touch; needs to receive a great deal of physical expressions of love; fears rejection and will say and do things knowing they are not right, but will do them to keep from being rejection; adopts behaviors of others; suffers from anxiety if told they are not loved, needed or appreciated; highly emotional; very inspiring, uplifting and loving.

Studies on how the temperaments affect spiritual growth, was done by Drs. Arno. These studies revealed that due to the "blending of temperaments"[30] the spiritual growth in individuals will be different. In order for a client to reach a closer relationship with God, he must first learn and understand his temperament.

---

[30] Ibid 57

"There are strengths and weakness with each temperament."[31] In Creation Therapy, we learn that the strengths are the way one may obtain and reach great goals in life. An example of this is when a person uses his strength to make their life better and the lives of those around them. A sign of weakness in temperament is when a person does the very things that they may hate that others do.

Temperament and Birth Order

The effect of birth order on behavior cannot be measured or scored, but it can be understood by the counselor. The birth order of the child has such an effect on the temperaments that the traits taken on by the child remain with them long after they've reached adulthood and leaves the immediate family. This is most true with the first born child. Normally, parents expecting the first child tend to get everything new.

Beginning with the first word to little league, cheerleading, piano lessons, high school and college, the child is pushed to be the best and to achieve the most. If the child's temperament thrives under this type of pressure, they will grow up to become independent, always reaching for that achievement. If not, they will want to achieve and try to please someone; however, he or she will feel as if they will never measure up.

---

[31] Ibid 59

When the middle child comes along, the parents know what they are doing. Although the child will be doing all of the above, these things are new to the child but not the parent. The middle child will most likely develop behavior traits totally different from the first child, and will always search for their own unique place for themselves. The uniqueness of this position is that the child is left to develop their own temperament because of less interference from the parents.

The parents have mellowed out and are pretty tired by the time the last child comes along. Whatever this child does, it is not as exciting as it was with the older siblings. This child will soon learn that in order to receive the attention and time they need, they will resort to drastic actions. This becomes a problem because by this time, the parents know this is the end of the line, so they may, without realizing it, they may be discouraging the child from leaving the home and becoming an adult.

Chapter Three
A BASIC UNDERSTANDING OF PAIN

According to Merriam-Webster Dictionary, pain is described as "acute mental or emotional distress or suffering." [32] Clients who come into CHMCLACC come to the center to address issues in dealing with their emotional pain. In order to get over painful situations, one must first understand the root of the pain, or what is causing it. Pain can come in many forms. One can experience emotional distress after a divorce, loss of job or loved one, etc. Some may even begin to suffer bouts of depression and withdrawal from their daily activities. One of the first steps taken at CHMCLACC is to help the client to differentiate between physical and emotional, which will assist the counselor in addressing and managing the pain.

The Web version of the Encyclopedia Britannica defines pain as "an experience consisting of a physiological (bodily) response to a noxious stimulus followed by an affective (emotional) response to that event."[33] It's interesting to notice that the Encyclopedia does not mention personal, private or perception. One must realize that emotional pain involves the mind.

---

[32] Merriam-Webster Dictionary 11th Ed.

[33] Encyclopaedia Brittanica Online. Encyclopaedia Britannica, 2001. Web. http://www.britannica.com/EBchecked/topic/438450/pain. (accessed 1 May 2011) (Above Emotional pain...)

Emotional pain takes many forms whether it results from stress and anxiety, grieving from the loss of a loved one, feeling as if one is stuck or trapped, regret, anger, etc. Normally, most folks will do their best to cope with these situations by holding it in and trying to act as if everything is normal. According to many clients that have come through the doors of CHMCLACC, they have all taken this approach thinking that it would be better to keep these feelings to themselves in order to not burden their family, friends and loved ones. However, the more they hold onto these feelings, the worse off they become. Clients are taught to address all aspects of their lives, what they have experienced, what they may have witnessed or heard that affects their personal lives.

Paraphrasing Shahar, who states "if we inject water into a clogged pipeline, the pressure will increase more if it were allowed to freely flow, but if the pressure continues to build, it can lead the pipeline to break and burst; unreleased painful feelings can lead to emotional breakdown."[34] If a client refuses to let go of their pain, it will eventually become more than they can handle. This type of pain can affect them physically as well as emotionally.

---

[34] Tal Ben Shahar *The Pursuit of Perfect: How to Stop Chasing Perfection and Start Living a Richer, Happier Life* (NY: McGraw Hill Books, 2009), 45-46.

Holding on to the old can be damaging in the new. "Find positive meanings in your situation and use whatever is at your disposal to improve solutions."[35] It may seem easier to hold on to the bad, but if clients will take this same energy and "give up trying to change it – it's history, and put 100 percent into creating a more skillful future,"[36] they will be able to move beyond the hurt and get to the other side of their pain.

Pain is a necessity for growth and development in everyone's life. No matter how a person lives his life, be it Christian or not, he will suffer at one point from emotional pain. No one is immune. This is all a part of God's plan. What clients also must realize is it is them who actually benefits from their pain. One may ask how this is so? Number one, it tests their faith. It teaches them to lean not on man, but to lean on Jesus. It also puts them in the position to assist others who may be experiencing emotional pain. Jesus feels the same pain that his brethren feels. "For we have not an high priest which cannot be touched with the feeling of our infirmities; but in all points tempted like as we are, yet without sin. (Hebrews 4:15).

---

[35] Joan Borysenko *It's Not the End of the World: Developing Resilience in Times of Change* (Australia: Hay House, 2009), 130.

[36] _____. Ibid. 129.

"The governing principles of the Compass work on the same conditions as the traditional compass. When we can establish where magnetic north can we establish what is east, south or west."[37] The main thing a person should realize that using north as the main direction, gives them a starting point as to which direction they need to go in working toward moving past the bad times in their life.

In Dr. Dye's *Joy In the Midst of Mourning*, she touches on the emotion of shock and teaches that "shock is one of the emotions that many people find hard to leave."[38] The state of shock allows one to deny what is actually happening in their life. However, once the shock wears off, and it will, it is then that the client must face what has happened and deal with those feelings accordingly. In most cases, after much counseling, the client learns how to accept the reality and move on. Emotions must have a way to be relieved, but it is a journey that must be taken in order to get to the other side.

---

[37] BenShea, Noah. *A Compass for Healing: Finding Your Way from Emotional Pain to Peace*. (Deerfield Beach FL: Health Communications Inc., 2006), 11.

[38] Dye, Dorothy. *Joy In the Midst of Mourning*. (2003) 2.

Sometimes, clients won't allow themselves to let go of painful experiences in the past. They carry them day after day, month after month, year after year. It never gets better. As Dimitrius states "Our subconscious holds thousands of experiences as a computer store information; however we can hit the 'find" button and instantly retrieve, but our subconscious is more haphazard if we weren't paying attention when the information was loaded."[39] Unless clients take notice of what they allow themselves to mentally hold on to, there's no telling what demons they are carrying. Sometime, they will continually put off what needs to be done. According to Basco "procrastination is a roadblock on your life path. It slows your progress and sometimes, takes you off course all together."[40] She goes on to say that "your improved self-awareness will put you in a stronger position to make changes that last."[41]

---

[39] Jo-Ellen Dimitrius, Mark Mazzarlla *Reading People: How to Understand People and Predict Their Behavior Anytime, Any Place* (NY: Random House, 1998) 216.

[40] Monica Ramiraz Basco *The Procrastinator's Guide to Getting Things Done* (NY: Guilford Press, 2010), 2.

[41] ____. Ibid, 18

Clients learn that there is a balance in life that must be met, such as with nature. Take for instance, the client may plant a garden but without water and nurturing, that garden cannot grow. The same goes for life's lessons. Pain is not there to sadden a person or make them feel bad, but it is there to make one aware that something is not right. It makes one aware that there may be something going on in their life that needs to be addressed. No matter how big or small. Most would prefer to go through life without experiencing negative or painful emotions, but this is impossible because pain is a part of life. "Pain in your life completes the purpose of God for your life."[42] In order for one to have a complete life, pain is a process that one must learn to accept when it happens, acknowledge that it's there and take the necessary steps in overcoming it.

Many times, clients have asked the question "Will I ever get over this?" According to Joyce Meyer, "Healing of emotional wounds is a process and not something that can happen overnight or all at once....it requires investing time and obedience to the commands of God."[43] This is something that is required of the clients at CHMCLACC. They must set aside time to spend with God and in His Word. They are taught to take a deep look into their lives and "examine your real self by enhancing self-awareness and understanding what you can do as well as what you can't...accept your strengths and limitations and realize they contribute to who you are, but are not the sole determinant of who you can become."[44]

---

[42] Dorothy Dye. *Joy In the Midst of Mourning*. 2003. 67

God desires to be a loving presence in our hearts. "As a brother to others, Jesus is present in our hopes and desires; this is the living and incarnate God that Jesus revealed to the people."[45] Sometimes, clients can be their own enemy. "When something phenomenal is happening in your life and you don't think you're good enough to have it, you will consciously or unconsciously find ways to sabotage it."[46] Too many times, a client may feel undeserving and may do everything in their power to ruin it or they may feel that the gift comes with some sort of condition that they will have to repay or return the favor. By "cultivating an attitude of acceptance and mindfulness,"[47] it will help clients accept the current situation and be mindful of what is going on within themselves or what is going on with those around them.

---

[43] Joyce Meyer. *Managing Your Emotions Instead of Your Emotions Managing You*. (Fenton, MI: Warner Books, 1997), 13.

[44] Bernardo J. Carducci, Susan Golant. *Shyness: A Bold New Approach: The Latest Scientific Findings Plus Practical Steps for Finding Your Comfort Zone*. (NY: Harper Collins Publishers, 2995), 146.

[45] http://edmundrice.net/index.php?option=com. Content&view-article$id=406:praying-with-out-hearts&catid=52;express-general&itemid=360. Accessed 3 March 2010

[46] Iyanla Vanzant *Peace from Broken Pieces: How to Get Through What You're Going Through* (NY: Smiley Books, 2010), 140.

[47] Richard O'Connor, *Happy at Last: The Thinking Person's Guide to Finding Joy* (NY: St. Martin's Press, 2008), 125.

There are two factors one must understand when it comes to pain and that it can be acute pain, which happens immediately, such as stubbing a toe. Although this type of pain may hurt right away, it soon will go away. When a person experiences the second type of pain, chronic, this pain may not be as hurtful, but it doesn't seem to go away. Counselors at CHMCLACC are taught to "recognize emotions in others depends on attentive listening and encouraging them to express their thoughts and feelings."[48]

There are times when two people may have come to counseling to address very similar issues in their lives. However, the outcome, although they each received the same type of counseling, the outcome can be totally different. The reason for this is because depending on how they were raised, the environments they were raised in, will all factor into how they receive assistance. If "Client A" was raised to ignore emotional pain, be strong, etc., it will take him a bit longer to adjust to the changes that he may feel goes against his upbringing. How many times have boys been told to "not cry," or "be strong," etc. Sadly, they take this advice into adulthood and never address their emotional pain. This can be very destructive because as the years go on, they have not taken any steps to get beyond the hurt and it becomes deeply rooted inside. The scary part about this is when it all comes to the forefront and can be quite destructive in the life of the client as well as his family and those around him. "Poorly managed emotions can create severe problems in relationships."[49]

---

[48] Lynn Clark, *SOS Help for Emotions: Managing Anxiety, Anger and Depression* (Bowling Green, KY: SOS Programs and Parent Press, 2002), 11.

In the instance of "Client B," who was raised to discuss and communicate issues, he was more accepting when it came to sitting down and communicating his problems. There was no fear that he would be made to look weak, such as what "Client A" was experiencing. Coming from a family that had an open communication policy, expressing his emotional pain came pretty easy for Client B. Raised by a strong, hard-working father, he was made aware that it's not considered a weakness when a man experiences emotional pain. His father taught him that it is okay for a man to cry. The problem arises when he tries to keep everything inside. This not only hurts him, but those around him because his entire attitude changes. He will tend to hurt those who are closest to him. Even though they are not responsible for his present state, they will be the ones to receive the outbursts, anger, etc.

Clients can be assured that no matter what they may be going through, they can be "confident and stand on, the Word of God, even in the midst of their pain."[50] God is always with His children. Even during the worst of times when He may feel as far away as the east is from the west. However, Psalm 34:3 states: "Even in spite of your pain, you can magnify the Lord because he is larger than any circumstance that you may be going through." Most clients don't realize this at the beginning of their sessions, but once they reach that point where they are beginning to see and feel the progress, it is this scripture that meant the most. It made them realize just how true it is.

---

[49] ____. Ibid. 11.

[50] Dorothy Dye. *Joy in the Midst of Mourning*. 2003. 63

In He-Motions, Bishop Jakes states that "reminding one's self of the truth about who you are and what you're about, and finding ways to remind yourself of this, will help with changing priorities, jobs, locations or lifestyles."[51] This can be an easy step to do. When the client feels that they are at their lowest, it helps a great deal if they remind themselves of what they have been blessed with, but also, to steer them in a more positive direction than what they are currently experiencing. And as John C. Maxwell says in Developing the Leader Within You, "people will not change until they perceive that the advantages of changing outweigh the disadvantages of continuing with the way things are."[52]

Many times, clients have come in complaining that their situations aren't supposed to be a certain way. According to Jeffers "when we let go of how it is supposed to be, we can relax and be more peaceful with the way it is."[53] Instead of clients dwelling on what they think their live is supposed to be, they are taught to accept what it is at the moment and deal with it accordingly. "When God sees you, He sees His son in you and the tremendous potential within your life."[54] God doesn't see His children the way they see themselves. He takes a deeper look at them and knows them through and through.

[51] T.D. Jakes *He-Motions: Even Strong Men Struggle* (NY: Putnam Printing, 2004), 51.

[52] John C. Maxwell, *Developing the Leader within You.* (Nashville, TN: Thomas Nelson Publishing, 1993), 58.

[53] Susan Jeffers *Embracing Uncertainty: Breakthrough Methods for Achieving Peace of Mind When Facing the Unknown* (NY: St. Martin's Press, 2003), 49.

One way to explain what happens at CHMCLACC is to tell the story of "Karen." Karen was raised in a fairly normal environment with both parents living in the home. Education was very important to Karen's parents, especially her father, because due to circumstances in his own life, he was unable to complete high school. Religion was also very important to her family. However, when Karen turned 18, she decided that she was an adult and could do whatever she wanted.

A few months before Karen turned nineteen, she met, as she would call him, "the man of my dreams." Being this was her first adult relationship, Karen jumped right into it. She believed everything this man told her and by the second year into their relationship, Karen gave birth to their first child. It was at this point that the man she thought she would spend the rest of her life with, walked out. With no support and too embarrassed to reach out to her family, she turned to alcohol. Before long, she had lost custody of her child.

This was very devastating to Karen, but by this time, she felt she was all alone and had no one to seek assistance from. She then lost her apartment. During the course of these actions, she met some friends who were into drugs. At this point, Karen felt as though she had nothing else to lose. She'd lost what she thought was the love of her life, her child was in foster care, and she was now homeless. It all started with experimenting with marijuana and eventually, ended with crack cocaine.

---

[54] Barbara Frederickson *Positivity* (NY: Crown Publishers, 2009), 119

For the next three and a half years, she went from pillar to post, crack house to crack house and, eventually, she ended up on the streets. Having no money or place to live, she began a life of prostitution—anything to feed her habit. She had to make enough money to get her next fix. She lasted all of five months on the streets before one of her "Johns" beat her badly. The anxiety of where she would get her next fix was much more than she was willing to deal with. To paraphrase Judith Viorst, "anxiety is painful, depression is painful....we may be powerless to prevent certain situations, but we can develop strategies to defend us against the pain...emotional detachment is one such defense."[55]

She ended up in the hospital fighting for her life. The day she was discharged, she got an elderly lady as a roommate. This woman took one look at her and knew that Karen needed help. On her way out of the hospital room, this woman stopped her, held her hand and quietly but sternly said: "Only He can help you." Karen knew exactly what this woman meant.

---

[55] Judith Viorst, *Necessary Losses: The Loves, Illusions, Dependencies and Impossible Expectations That All of Us Have to Give Up in Order to Grow* (NY: The Free Press: 2002), 32.

She stopped at the chapel, got down on her knees and let it all out. She prayed and cried, cried and prayed. She asked God to guide her and decided that she would put all of her trust in Him and not into drugs. It was this day that she walked into the Department of Social Services to request help. She eventually landed a spot in an in-house rehabilitation center. When she received this news, she felt a sense of peace come over her body. It was then that she knew God had heard her prayers. Every time she felt the urge to go back to her old ways, she'd remember that little old lady in the hospital room and knew what she needed was God. She began to have conversation after conversation with Him. At the time, she didn't know that He was working things out for her.

She finished her rehabilitation and began attending daily meetings, sometimes two or three a day. She also began to take parenting classes as well as job-training classes. She eventually got supervised visits with her child, and after the first visit she knew that she would do everything in her power to be the mother that she was meant to be. The next hardest thing she had to accomplish was to reestablish contact with her family. It had been almost two years since she'd spoken to anyone. This one was a big step for her because she thought they had given up on her and wanted nothing to do with her. But again, God stepped in and gave her the courage to make that call. The first call was to her grandmother, who told her that our hearts and homes will always be open to her, but she would have to do the right thing. She also told her to call her parents and, even if they are upset and angry, it was she who had to make the first step.

But again, as usual, God stepped in. As Joyce Meyer says in Power of a Simple Prayer, "When we roll our problems on God, He changes our thoughts and make them agree with His will."[56] Clients are made aware that God is and always will be in charge. If they make the necessary changes, give their burden to God, He will change our thought patters according to His will. However, unless the client is willing to surrender to God, the problems will continue day after day, year after year.

She was amazed at the love and concern that her parents showed her during that call. Yes, they were disappointed in her choices, but they would always be her parents, and she would always be their daughter. Two weeks after that phone call, Karen was back at home with the people who loved her and was eventually reunited with her child. When the pastor finally saw Karen, and they had the chance to sit down and talk, the very first thing she said was "If it weren't for the power of prayer, I know I would be dead." She was asked her to elaborate on this, and she recounted the story of the little old lady in her hospital room. She said she reminded her of her grandmother, and it was at that moment that she remembered that her grandmother always said that no matter what happens in your life, the answer can always be found in the Bible.

---

[56] Joyce Meyer. *Power of a Simple Prayer: How to Talk with God About Everything*. New York. FaithWords. 2007. 120

Although Karen had been clean from the drugs and the street life, she still felt a though she was not emotionally stable to continue on this walk. She began counseling sessions at CHMCLACC where she was made to go back to the time in her life that she felt things started to get out of control. She relayed that her life was pretty normal, but for some reason, she thought her parents were too strict on her. Many of her friends were able to do whatever it was they wanted. They didn't have curfews to abide by, nor were they required to attend church. It was at this point in her life that she felt that they were trying to control her. However, she began to realize through counseling that the rules her parents set for her, the very rules that she broke many times over, were to keep her from the life in which she ended up living.

Karen had to learn how to forgive before she could move on. She had to forgive herself because "real forgiveness means looking steadily at the sin, the sin that is leftover without excuses, after all allowances has been made, and seeing it in its dirt, meanness and malice and reconciling to the person who has done it."[57] In this instance, she had to forgive herself. "Forgive our trespass as we forgive those who trespass against us. We are offered forgiveness on no other terms, to refuse it is to refuse God's mercy for ourselves."[58] God forgives all. She had to trust and believe that she was worth forgiving as well.

---

[57] C.L. Lewis *The Weight of Glory* (New York, NY: Harper Collins, 2001), 181

[58] ____. 183

The first thing Karen realized that she needed to do was accept that her parents were right and she was wrong. She realized that during those early years, she thought she was going to prove her parents wrong. However, she just proved that they were absolutely right in setting down those rules. It was at this point during the counseling sessions that she also realized that in order for her to be totally successful in overcoming her personal situation, she had to go back home and speak to her parents, apologize for her actions and most importantly, acknowledge that it was because of the choices that she made, that she ended up having to experience the consequences of those choices. Karen was finally able to understand that her pain didn't originate from the man, alcohol, drugs, homelessness, etc., but from her wanting to be an adult before she was mature enough to handle an adult life. She had to learn that once she found herself "locked in the vise grip, breaking the habit sounded difficult, but its straightforward when you learn to notice when it's happening and redirecting your focus."[59] She had to

---

[59] Stephen Ilardi *The Depression Cure: The 6-Step Program to Beat Depression without Drugs* (Cambridge, MA: Da Capo Press, 2009), 94.

Karen didn't feel as though she was abandoned anymore. Even though she is the one that left, she didn't realize how much of an impact that decision would have on her family. Marilynne Robinson states, "then there is the matter of my mother's abandonment of me again, this is the common experience. They walk ahead of us, they are lost in the thought of their own and sooner or later, they disappear...the only mystery is that we expect it to be otherwise."[60] Sadly, sometimes we know what the true outcome of situations are, but will prefer to believe it will be the opposite.

Another aspect of counseling people going through pain is for them to take a look at their immediate environment. Looking at some of the clients at CHMCLACC, it was found that the way in which they were raised also played a major role in how they dealt with painful situations. Ironically, for the men who participated in counseling sessions, the majority had been raised with the false belief that men are to be strong, or men who show emotions are weak. These unfounded reasons have hindered many men from overcoming their pain. They did not want to look weak to their families. However, by not addressing their situations, it only made them worse.

---

[60] Marilynne Roinson *Housekeeping* (NY: Bantam Books, 1982), NP

Clients and counselees of CHMCLACC will learn to decipher between which emotions they are experiencing. If they are anger, anger is addressed. If they are hurt, hurt is addressed. Clients are taught to deal only with the emotion that is causing them grief, anxiety, etc. However, not only is their emotional being addressed, but also, anything surrounding it that may play a part in their feelings. For example, if "John" is depressed because he is about to lose his home to foreclosure, not only will he meet with the counselor, but he will also have the chance to meet with a real estate lawyer to explain the foreclosure process. Many times, people find themselves in situations and they have no clue how they got there. They have been so used to just taking the word of the real estate agent, etc. and not learn the process themselves. By teaching clients the basic rules and regulations in situations such as the foreclosure, it gives the client a better understanding of how the entire process works.

    Dr. Orloff found that "Achieving emotional freedom gives you ongoing access to your own power center during jubilant times and in adversity. As master of your emotions, you'll have the where withal to hold your own with angels, demons and everything in between."[61]. Dr. Orloff said, she admires your courage in getting to know yourself. The journey to self-knowledge is an exhilarating yet humbling one. As it unfolds, keep distilling the core message of emotional freedom: Outer events may be the stimulus for an upset, but how you choose to respond determines your experience"

    [61] Judith Orloff, *Emotional Freedom. Liberate Yourself from Negative Emotions and Transform Your Life:* NY: Harmony books, 2009), 374.

Emotional Pain

The claim is emotional pain will always grow deeper unless you allow God to be in control. Joyce Meyer wrote "many people are hurting so badly and they are crying out for help and the problem is they are not willing to receive the help they need from God."[62]

One may think it's difficult to accept the help that they are in need of. A lot of this stems from having false pride. They are too embarrassed or feel the need to conquer their pain by themselves.

This is accepted by "the truth is, no matter how much we may want or need help, we are never going to receive it until we are willing to do things the way God wants us to."[63] John 14:6 is evidence supporting this when Jesus said: "I am the way." Ms. Meyers further explains "He (God) has His own way of doing things, and by allowing ourselves to decrease in self and increase in Him, all things will begin in the process of getting to the other side of pain and if you receive emotional healing, you must learn to do so in the face of truth."[64]

During the course of counseling sessions at CHMCLACC, the clients must be willing to "rejoice in the problem, not for, but in the problem because God uses it for good in our lives."[65]

---

[62] Joyce Meyer. *Managing Your Emotions Instead of Your Emotions Handling You*. Fenton, Missouri. 1997. 51

[63] Ibid. 51

[64] Ibid., 65

[65] Rick Warren *God's Power to Change Your Life* (Grand Rapids, MI: Zondervan, 1990), 73.

According to Joyce Meyer, "Healing of emotional wounds is a process and not something that can happen overnight or all at once. This type of healing requires investing time and obedience to the commands of God."[66] Counselees participating in therapy at CHMCLACC are taught that emotional pain can be caused by the everyday stresses that may occur in life. Once they realize this, it makes it much easier to address their problems. One way clients are advised in handling emotional pain is to share these experiences with others. Everyone handles emotional pain different so there is no "correct" was when dealing with this type of pain.

In order for a client to break the cycle of pain, they must first accept that they are going through an emotional period and not be made to feel embarrassed when seeking out help to overcome it. When a person does not receive what they want, they tend to get emotional whether it be the feeling of rejection or hurt. This type of feelings will alter the way a person may act and/or react. Some clients that have come through CHMCLACC think that they must have everything they want in life in order to be happy. However; according to life's experiences, this is not a true statement. From listening to counselees, the more they had, the more they seemed to want, which in turn, proves that no matter what one may have in life, they will still experience some sort of painful situation.

---

[66] Joyce Meyer, *Managing Your Emotions*. 13

"Some emotional pain, with time, will leave. But sometimes, a person will continuously live with this pain because they are not willing to let it go or at other times, they may not be able."[67] Even during the process of going through emotional pain, God can and will help through this process. However, according to Dr. Dorothy Dye, "pain is normal in everyone's life, but being in Christ gives you another perspective."[68]

Additional evidence is found in the word of God "….if you abide in my word, hold fast to my teachings and live in accordance with them, you are truly my disciples and you will know the truth and the truth will set you free." (John 8:31-32). Ms. Meyers reveals that "the truth is always revealed through the Word, but people don't always accept it."[69] Many times clients have heard the saying that truth hurts. This is a very true statement. However, when a client is focusing on their walk with Christ and overcoming difficult situations, the truth is something many refuse to acknowledge. But by doing so, they are hindering their growth in Christ and their success in overcoming their emotional pain.

---

[67] http://www.hubpages.com/hub/Dealing-With-Your-Emotional-Pain. Accessed 29 January 2010.

[68] Dorothy Dye. *Joy in the Midst of Mourning*. 2003. 11

[69] Joyce Meyer *Battlefield of the Mind* (NY: Faith Words, 1995), 23.

Joyce Meyers also stated that "when you are having emotional problems, one of the things I encourage you to do is to realize the emotions you are experiencing are not the problem, but only its manifestation."[70] This explains how one may allow a situation to change their emotions such as experiencing the loss of a job. This will cause a person to become worried, depressed, anxious, etc. What you need to do is not just deal with the symptoms, your emotions, but to get at the root of the problem. Whatever it is that is causing you to feel the way you do."[71] This is the moment the counselor should address how the counselee can get back out in the workforce in the case of a job loss. By helping them to reach out to other avenues, it gives the counselee a way to overcome the pain from their job loss as well address the pain itself.

According to Phillips, "most problems classified as a form of mental illness are in reality:
   1) Broken Relationships
   2) Unfulfilled or unrealized expectations of life
   3) Guilt over not doing what we should do
   4) Disobedience
   5) Inability to adjust to and accept hurtful experiences
   6) Unwilling to let go of the past and forgive others
   7) Low self-image or high, perfectionist standards."[72]

---

[70] Joyce Meyers, *Managing Your Emotions Instead of Your Emotions Handling You.* (Fenton, Missouri. 1997) 85.

[71] Ibid., 85.

The above list shows that these problems can be the root of what's really going on in a client's life. Certain aspects will have negative effects on a person's mental being and emotions. By looking at all avenues of the client's life, what's going on around them, in their households or on their jobs, it will allow the counselor to get to the very root of the client's problem and at this point, make the necessary changes to address them.

CHMCLACC's objective is to get to the root of the problem. It believes by addressing the root and the unnecessary side effects, the pain can be alleviated. However; when the energy is focused on a symptom, it is usually addressed with medication. The beliefs at CHMCLACC, based on the hundreds of cases that have come through their center, it was discovered that by dealing directly with the root of the problem and addressing the whole situation, clients gain another perspective of their situations and are able to move in the direction to better understand themselves and their circumstances.

Worshipping Through Pain

---

[72] Bob Phillips *Controlling Your Emotions Before They Control You:* (Eugene, OR: Harvest House Publishers, 1995), 31.

What is worship? According to Merriam-Webster's Collegiate Dictionary, worship is defined as "reverence offered a divine being as well as the act of expressing such reverence."[73] In Called to Worship, written by Vernon Whaley, he states "We must read the word of God. Worship is our response to God's Revelation, and God reveals Himself in His word."[74] Clients are made aware that if they take the time to get to know God, to stay in His word, it will be an asset in helping them to move forward in their lives and overcome painful situations. The Bible has stories that one can use in everyday life.

When a person decides to take their burdens to God, they must realize that until they surrender fully, they will continue to meet obstacles. Too many times, people think that they can "help" God. God needs no help! As the old saying goes, "if you want to make God laugh, tell him your plans." God is a restorer. He can heal our every hurt. When His children are hurting, God is hurting also. He does not want His children to experiencing unnecessary pain and wants all of His children to come unto Him. But there are many times people will put up a resistance because they have not taken the time to study the word of God. The most important aspect when one decides to worship God is to surrender. Don't worry about the "what ifs," or what could have or should have been. God is and will always be in control.

---

[73] Merriam-Webster Collegiate Dictionary, 11th Ed.

[74] Vernon Whaley. *Called to Worship*. (Nashville, Thomas Nelson, 2009), 334.

"True worship is dependent now on a person, not a place; on Jesus, not the temple. The time has come because Jesus has come."[75] This statement from True Worship, by Vaughn Roberts tells us that while worshiping through painful situations, one should concentrate on Jesus, not the church or venue in which we are praying. The counselors on staff at CHMCLACC are taught to stand by their clients to help sort through any issues they may be experiencing. As in Called to Counsel, the "ultimate goal is to assist the counselee to come into agreement with God about the healing He has for them."[76]

---

[75] Vaughn Roberts. *True Worship*. GA. Authentic Lifestyle. 2002. 5.

[76] John R. Cheydleur. *Called to Counsel*. IL. Tyndale House Publishing Inc. 1999. 172.

"Every individual has the ability, through healing prayers, to express faith – the belief in the truth, value, or trustworthiness of a person, idea, or things. It goes on to say that 'Biblical faith is determined by reliance upon God rather than man and confidence in the power of God"[77] When a person makes the decision to put his faith in God, he or she will begin not only to feel, but see the power of God's work. God will be there to help you make the necessary changes needed so that things will be according to His Will, just as the scripture reads: "....for I will turn their mourning into joy, and will comfort them, and make them rejoice from their sorrow." (Jeremiah 31:13 NKJV). This scripture is telling God's children that if they will turn to Him, He will give them the comfort that they need. God will turn their sorrow into joy. He has promised that if you bring your grief and sorrow to Him, His promises, you will receive. Even when one may be suffering, God is fulfilling His promises and purpose for their life.

---

[77] http://www.allaboutprayer.org/healing-prayers.htm. Accessed 2 January 2010

Ms. Meyer points out that one should "realize that the emotions one may be experiencing are not the problem, but only its manifestation."[78] A counselor must help the client to get to the root of the problem by addressing what is causing it. Some emotional problems stem from separation from a job, relationship, family, etc. and until those issues are addressed, it will be difficult to be successful in overcoming the emotional pain that results in these situations. She goes on to say that a person must be "willing to open up ourselves and allow the Holy Spirit to come in and cleanse us from within and one will find themselves coming into better fellowship with those around them."[79]

One important aspect of worshiping through pain is "while worshiping, we should worship God in the spirit of God Himself because it's His spirit that dwells within us."[80] Dr. Whaley teaches us in Dynamics of Corporate Worship that it is "essential in understanding the priority of prayer is to pray expectantly."[81]

Prayer Will Bring A Change

---

[78] Joyce Meyer, *Managing Your Emotions Instead of Your Emotions Managing You* (Fenton, MI: Warner Books, 1997), 85.

[79] Ibid., 84.

[80] Vernon Whaley *Called to Worship* (Nashville, TN: Thomas Nelson, 2009), 253.

[81] ____ . *The Dynamics of Corporate Worship 2nd Ed.* (Virginia Beach, VA: Academix Publishing Services Inc., 2009), 137.

"Elias was a man subject to passions as we are, and he prayed earnestly that it might not rain; and it rained not on the earth by the space of three years and six months. And he prayed again, and the heaven gave rain, and the earth brought forth her fruit." (James 5:17-18 NKJV). Prayer is the one thing that everyone on this earth has, if they take advantage of it. Everyone, believers and non-believers, have uttered a prayer, whether or not they realize it or not. Prayer is really just having a conversation with God. Sometimes, one may think God does not hear their prayers. However, Christians are taught to believe that God hears all prayers. The problem arises when one thinks God has not answered these prayers. The truth of the matter is, God answers all prayers. However, the problem lies when one may feel that God did not give them the answer they were hoping for.

"Call unto me and I will answer thee, and show thee great and mighty things, which thou knoweth not." (Jeremiah 33:3. Bishop Hilliard wrote, "If you will commit to pray, your prayer time will become a special time where God will begin to reveal things to you that are critical to your destiny and quality of life."[82] The reason this point of view is accepted is CHMCLACC considers the methods God uses to convey His message. There is always the chance that one may doubt if their prayers are effective. Nonetheless, God is directing our life to understand certain things. However; one must know that God's word is where he should look for comfort and the ability to be overwhelmed by the peace that God will allow in their life "along with this peace comes a knowing and confidence that a person never experienced before. Prayer is powerful."[83].

Farber wrote, "The Supreme Court has dealt gingerly with the topic of the right to die, and any recognition of this right must be tempered with the appreciation of the potential problems. The government clearly has the right to block decisions caused by mental illness, lack of information, or undue pressure. When the person is incapacitated, careful procedures are warranted to determine his or her true wishes. But at the end of the day, the Ninth Amendment does not allow the government to impose its views on unwilling citizens."[84]

---

[82] I.V. Hilliard *Secret For a Better Life. Simple Strategies to Improve the Quality of Your Life Today.* (Houston, TX. New Spectrum Media Concept. 2007). 114.

[83] Ibid. 114.

Through the process of change in the lives of clients, this is one example of the road blocks that they find is blocking them from getting to the other side of pain. Everyone has the constitutional right to be free of some things and protected by others. They have the right to move past the present pain. However; there are always outside entities that stand in the way of moving past one painful experience to another.

This is a clear example of having something in your life but because of limited knowledge, a person may become stuck in their situations and unable to move past one freedom to another. Therefore, we know that the dream of peace, the peace that surpasses all understanding, can be met. It is the peace that will measure the comfort in working through the present issue. The process will prepare the client for the road ahead. The pain of not getting or having what you are entitled to will also hinder one's growth to getting to the other side.

---

[84] Daniel Farber. *Retained by the People, The "Silent" Ninth Amendment and the Constitutional Rights Americans Don't Know They Have.* New York. Basic Books. 2007. 121

Bishop Jakes wrote, "For many men, it's necessary to come to this place of abasement, to wake up the morning after, to see the evidence of indiscretion or consequences of your addiction, to see your reflection leaning over the pig's trough."[85] We take this to mean that we have all fallen short of God's expectations, but this is when we must pray to Him in earnest to achieve the goals of getting past these discretions. He goes on to say that "while it can be a time as confusing as being lost after midnight in the foggy country road without your GPS system, you must learn to navigate, to ask for direction, if necessary (something men find impossible to do), to make a U-turn and redirect your vehicle's destination."[86] Sometimes, it's okay to change the plan. Nothing is ever set in stone. This is the time to look deeply at the plan we may have made and make the necessary changes to move in the right direction.

Bishop Jakes goes on further to say "you must be willing to get comfortable with the journey of your life and quite waiting for life to begin when you reach a certain destination, even the failed choices and wrong turns can be redeemed by God if you're willing to let Him."[87] What we take from this quote is although the situation may not be the one chosen, but in order to get past it, one must be comfortable in that situation in order to deal with it properly.

---

[85] T.D. Jakes, *He-Motions: Even Strong Men Struggle*. New York: Penguin Group. 2004 22.

[86] Ibid., 22.

[87] Ibid., 22.

In moving to the other side of pain, Bishop T.D. Jakes wrote "it is only in the understanding that we may learn to heal our own wounds; men are aching inside, souls are trembling with anger and hurt and sorrow and our hearts yearning for our embrace, the scent of his cologne or the spotlight of his attention."[88] Sometimes, folks may wait and wait and before they realize it, it's too late and "the clock has run out and they are left to find comfort in surrogate fathers and other male relationships."[89] Therefore, the process needs to begin in order to understand the level of pain. The pain needs to be revealed in order to grow through the healing process.

CHMCLACC has made it a commitment to God that it would be placed in an arena known as "Pro Deo," and this duty to God will not wager on the elements that are needed to encourage, empower or provoke one to move past their present state of mind.

"Love God in the tensions and contradictions."[90] Even though this may be hard for some to do, a person must be willing to continue to show love to God because if it weren't for God, that person may not even be here to go through the bad time. This is the time to praise Him the most. He will never forsake us. God is with His children through everything they may go through in life, the good and the bad. Just hold onto His words and He will see you through.

---

[88] Ibid., 109.

[89] Ibid., 109.

[90] Rick Mathis. The *Christ Centered Heart: Peaceful Living in Difficult Times*.(MI: Liguori/Triumph, 1999). 48.

In Psalm 6 was written by David when he was experiencing a great deal of physical pain. He suffered greatly from the lack of sleep, his bones ached and he was surrounded by his enemies. David thought that God had forgotten or abandoned him because he had been angry with God. There are times in life that one may have experienced the very same thing David experienced. There are days when one may feel that what can go wrong, will go wrong.

Prayer changes things in different ways such as when Peter raised Tabitha from death. "But Peter put them all forth, and kneeled down, and prayed; and turning him to the body said, 'Tabitha, arise.' And she opened her eyes; and when she saw Peter, she sat up." (Acts 9:40 KJV). This would be considered a miracle. However, most prayers are answered in a pretty ordinary manner such as one may pray for a new job, new home, financial blessing, etc. God answers them all.

In the story of David, he was so upset with God that he felt God was too far from him. But instead of David being angry, he decided to change his prayer and stop complaining. This is where he began to rely on his faith and says "Depart from me, all ye workers of iniquity; for the Lord hath heard the voice of my weeping. The Lord hath heard my supplication; the Lord will receive my prayer." (Psalm 6:8-9 KJV).

During a session with a client, the client confessed to the counselor at CHMCLACC that it was much easier to worship God when he had everything he wanted in life. However, he felt it very difficult to worship when he was going through tough times. Like many people, he asked himself "why would God allow me to suffer?" He never once realized that through these sufferings, he became a stronger man. He only concentrated on the pain. Instead of blaming God, he was made aware during counseling sessions that he should have been thanking God. He was very confused because he thought that it would be silly to be thankful for something so painful. But over the course of his sessions, he came to realize that because of God, he was truly blessed. Because he had come to know God, he then realized that over the course of his life, he will experience painful situations. This is just a given. No one is immune. All one has to do is look at what Jesus went through to save the world of their sins.

Sadly, many people, when they are rewarded with something that they've been wanting, the first thing they think is they got lucky. Luck has nothing to do with it, but God does. "Every person has the ability, through healing prayers, to express faith – the belief in the truth, value or trustworthiness of a person, idea or thing."[91] When a person makes a purchase, they have faith that whatever they bought, it will do what it's supposed to do, whether it is a car, television, etc. When a man goes to the barber, he has faith that the barber knows what he is doing. "Faith is the substance of things hoped for, the evidence of things not seen." (Hebrews 11:1 KJV). One must be willing to rely on God instead of man. Too many times, folks today will look toward their pastor, preacher, rabbi, etc. to be the one who'll change their lives. But like the grieving father whose daughter had just died, prayed to Jesus and was told "not to be afraid….to just believe."[92] It is then that Jesus takes the hand of the child and restores her.

When Jesus was on earth, he came into contact with many, many people. Some who were dealing with faith issues, asked his followers to pray and to never lose heart. By this, he meant for people to open their hearts and allow God to enter. It's one thing to "think" that God is working in an individual's life however; it's a totally different feeling when one can feel God's presence in our lives.

---

[91] http://www.allaboutprayer.org/healing-prayers.htm. Accessed 2 January 2010.

[92] Ibid

At CHMCLACC, the counselees and clients are given a simple assignment, which helps bring them closer to God. When the client is dealing with painful emotions, instead of dwelling on that pain, clients are taught that when these feelings arise, to pray. Every time they may start to feel low, unappreciated, rejected, to not claim those negative feelings but to get down on their knees and pray to God. While working on achieving a peace of mind, one should remember that Paul "tells us to pray for peace because of God's desire that all be saved and come to know the truth."[93] Prayer is sometimes, all that a person may have left. God wants all of His children to be comfortable in coming to Him. Prayer, in general, is just having a conversation with God. It's really not hard at all. All one has to do is open his mouth and speak. God will hear their cries.

According to Drs. Clinton and Sibcy in *Why You Do the Things You Do*, "if you allow it to happen, relationships with God satisfies all conditions when we seek him."[94] In essence, what they are saying is to simply, go to God. Take your cares and burdens to Him and allow His Will to be done. Bishop T.D. Jakes states that "one of the greatest challenges of our walk with God is to resist the temptation to allow what has happened in the past to determine who we are today."[95] Clients realize during their sessions that because they may have done something in their past, it doesn't define who they are today. Everyone makes bad choices, but it doesn't mean they are bad people.

---

[93] John Piper. *Let the Nations Be Glad: The Supremacy of God in Missions*. (Grand Rapids, MI: Baker Academic, 1993), 50.

[94] Tim Clinton and Gary Sibcy, *Why You Do the Things You Do: The*

Bishop Jakes goes on to say that "God is able to repair the broken places, but it requires us to expose where those places are. and if man hides from God, he loses himself."[96]

In 2Corinthians 1:3-4 KJV, the scripture says "Blessed be God, even the Father of our Lord Jesus Christ, the Father of mercies, and the God of all comfort; Who comforteth us in all our tribulation, that we may be able to comfort them which are in any trouble, by the comfort wherewith we ourselves are comforted of God." One can learn much from this scripture. For example, if the counselor has lost a parent and is counseling a client in the same position, the counselor can honestly say: "I understand how you feel." However, because everyone's grief is different, the counselor "cannot say he knows how the counselee feels because everyone's relationship with their parents are different, which in turn means their emotional perspective will be different as well.[97]

Secret to Healthy Relationships. (Nashville, TN: Thomas Nelson Publisher, 2006), 129.

[95] T.D. Jakes *Naked and Not Ashamed* (PA: Destiny Image Publishers, 1995), 47.

[96] ____. Ibid. 8-9.

[97] Dorothy Dye. *Joy In the Midst of Mourning.* 63.

In an article found on caringinfo.org, "pain should be taken seriously and treated with dignity and respect by healthcare professionals."[98] Many counselees are already feeling a bit shy or reluctant to seek help but if they are met with unprofessionalism or doubt by those who are supposed to help them; it makes this process more difficult to address. The counselee feels as though he is just taking up time, or that their problems may not be worth it. One important aspect that clients have and are made aware of at CHMCLACC is that no matter what is offered, they have the right to accept or refuse the type of treatment offered to them.

Chapter Four
PREPARATIONS FOR GETTING PAST THE PAIN
Make Jesus Your Best Friend And Rock

What is a friend: "Friend is one attached to another by affection or esteem; one that is not hostile, of the same nation, party or group; one that favors or promote something (as in charity) or favored company. To be a favored is to treat gently or carefully, do a kindness for and give support or confirmation; to afford advantage for success to grow."[99]

---

[98] http://www.caringinto.org/i4a/pages/index.cfm?pageid=3349. Accessed 26 December 2009

[99] Encyclopedia Bitannica Company Merriam-Webster.

This is easier than most people think. Sometimes when we go through trials and tribulations, we will go to everyone else first. Be it a brother or sister, friend, spouse, or coworker. But until Jesus is put first, one can never understand the true love that He bestows upon all of His children. However, sometimes one must get to the lowest point before realizing that pain is not wanted in our lives. A person will dread the situations that they anticipate will be painful. Many times, they even pray to be spared any and all painful experiences. But not only will they survive the pain, they will also profit from it.

Sometimes, it seems as though the pain may stretch to the limits, forcing one to look for guidance from others, and it pushes them to consider new choices. Pain is the common denominator as members of the human family. It softens people to others, it fosters empathy, and it helps one to reach out and realize their need for one another. New knowledge and new awareness are additional benefits of accepting, rather than denying, the pain that accompanies life. This journey will move one further along the path of enlightenment. One can consider that each problem, each crisis that arises, is necessary in our preparation for moving forward.

"God desires for us to know His will more than we want to know it."[100] God has written His words, has sent His son for us to get to know. The one thing that's amazing is how simple it is to receive Him. All a person has to do is be willing to accept Him and live according to His laws.

[100] T.D. Jakes. *Power for Living*. (Shippenburg, PA: Destiny Image Publisher, 1995). 86.

Even though a person may be fearful of the new, one must go forward. It's comforting to remember that as long as they have Jesus, they never take any steps alone. It is one's destiny to experience many new steps as they overcome a painful experience and start a new beginning. Without the new beginnings, one is unable to fulfill the purpose for which God has created for them.

"What matters is that you commit to finding and reconnecting with your authentic self."[101] When the client realizes that they must be true to themselves first, it allows them to make the necessary step in working to overcome painful experiences in their lives. However, one thing they must understand and take into consideration is that they must not allow others to make them feel less than, or make them feel as if they are more important. It is critical for the client to be accepting of the person they are instead of being who others want them to be.

"Regardless of how horrible your circumstances, you are probably not paralyzed and unable to speak."[102] However, there are times when going through extremely difficult circumstances or situations, one may feel that they are paralyzed in the moment. Some folks will feel as though they are stuck and there's nothing they can do to overcome these situations or even worse, they know that something can be done, but have no idea how. And it's at this point where they seek out counseling.

---

[101] Phil McGraw. *Self Matters: Creating Your Life from the Inside Out.* (NY. Free Press, 2003), 288.

[102] Chuck Gallozzi, "Overcoming Adversity." http://www.personal-

By accepting the reality of the suffering one may have in his life, realizing that it is a part of God's plan helps in dealing with and being able to overcome this experience. Until a person accepts their suffering, they will not be able to deal with them or even more-so, overcome them. God has destined the lives of His children from the time they were in their mother's womb. His plan for their lives has already been written. But knowing that God will guide them through the most difficult times is the one positive and truth that a person can have.

Pain, suffering, stress, and other difficulties a person may face in their life is something that they should understand is just a part of their being. How many times has one thought that without the daily stress, life would be much better? But the bottom line is no matter what type of life one may be living, experiencing painful situations is a given. No one is immune. But, one must realize there is help and assistance out there. What type of world would we live in if everything was perfect? It is essential that pain be a part of life. Without pain, there can be no healing.

"As fellow members of the Body, we are challenged to call on the name of Jesus, who is our liberator and source of power, and to ask him to walk beside us as we seek help."[103] Jesus wants to be a friend to his brethren. All He asks is that you reach out to Him and He will be there every time He's needed.

---

devgelopment.com/chuck/adversity.htm. (accessed 12 December 2009).

[103] Neil Anderson, Terry Zuehkle, Julianne Zuehkle. *Christ Centered Therapy* (Grand Rapids, MI: Zondervan Publishing House, 2000). 340.

As Bishop T.D. Jakes states in *Naked and Not Ashamed*, "Emotional pain is to the spirit what physical pain is to the body...pain warns us that something is out of order and may require attention."[104] Too many times, clients have refused to listen to their bodies and try to go on as nothing is wrong. By doing this, they continue to suppress the very feelings that need to be addressed. The longer they ignore the warning signs, the longer and more difficult it will be to overcome the painful situation. Clients are taught to pay attention to what their bodies may be telling them. A headache could also mean there is something stressful going on in their lives that they need to take a look at and see where they can make the necessary steps to move past it.

Sometimes, we need to turn away from what's troubling us and turn it over to Jesus. Hanging onto a situation for which no solution is immediately apparent only exaggerates and prolongs the situation. It is said often that the solution to any problem lies within it. But when we keep turning the problem over and over in our minds, we keep the attention on the outer appearance, not the inner solution. However, when we rest, meditate, or put our attention to other matters, it opens the way for God to reveal the solution. Every problem we may face can be resolved through God. We need to be open to it. We need to step away from our ego and listen to words of encouragement through friends as well as to the words that come from within our own hearts.

---

[104] T.D. Jakes. *Naked and Not Ashamed: We've Been Afraid to Reveal What God Longs to Heal*. (NY: Putnam's Sons, 1999), 79.

Jesus is, and always has been, right there. All we had to do is ask. But many times, instead of going to Jesus first, He becomes our last resort. You will need to do four things faithfully every day so you will grow in God. How many times have we tried to solve our problems on our own? And how many of these times did we fail? Relying on God is foreign to many people. We were encouraged from early childhood to be self-reliant, and even when we desperately needed another's help, we feared asking for it. Once our confidence wavered, as it so often does, we hid the fear, sometimes with pills or alcohol. We sometimes just hid inside our homes. Then, after giving our pain over to Jesus, we realize that we never needed to fear anything, that God was never distant. Slowly and with practice, it will become natural to turn within, to be God-reliant rather than self-reliant.

I remember hearing my grandmother recite the following, which relays the message of having Jesus as a friend:

> What a friend we have in Jesus
> All our sins and grief to bear!
> What a privilege to carry
> Everything to God in prayer!
> Oh, what peace we often forfeit,
> Oh, what needless pain we bear,
> All because we do not carry
> Everything to God in prayer!
>
> Have we trials and temptations?
> Is there trouble anywhere?
> We should never be discouraged —
> Take it to the Lord in prayer.

Can we find a friend so faithful?
Who will all our sorrows share?
Jesus knows our every weakness;
Take it to the Lord in prayer.

Are we weak and heavy-laden?
Cumbered with a load of care?
Precious Savior, still our refuge
Take it to the Lord in prayer.
Do thy friends despise, forsake thee?
Take it to the Lord in prayer!
In His arms He'll take and shield thee,
Thou wilt find a solace there.

Blessed Savior, Thou hast promised
Thou wilt all our burdens bear;
May we ever, Lord, be bringing?
All to Thee in earnest prayer.
Soon in glory bright, unclouded,
There will be no need for prayer —
Rapture, praise, and endless worship,
Will be our sweet portion there.[105]

---

[105] Joseph Scriven, "What a Friend We Have in Jesus" http://library.timelesstruths.org/music/What_a_Friend_We_Have_in_Jesus/; accessed 17 December 2009.

Let's take a look at the first four lines of this song. What exactly is it relaying to us? To answer that, this song is telling us that Jesus is our friend and that we don't have to carry our burdens alone. He will carry our burdens for us, if we would just bring them to him in prayer. However, the next four lines explains that when we refuse to lean on Jesus, we are only hurting ourselves and we will forfeit the peace that He has for us by not allowing Him to shoulder our burdens. The last four lines tells us that when we go to the Lord in prayer, we will be blessed with eternal life, a glory bright and unclouded.

"And [so] the Scripture was fulfilled that says, Abraham believed in (adhered to; trusted in, and relied on) God, and this was accounted to him as righteousness (as conformity to God's will in thought and deed), and he was called God's friend. (James 2:23 Amplified). In the King James Version, this scripture reads: "And the scripture was fulfilled which saith, Abraham believed in God, and it was imputed unto him for righteousness; and he was called the Friend of God." In God's word, it is understood that you have to believe in Him in order for Him to be your friend. Believing in God the All Mighty will provide the peace and elements in getting to the other side of pain. As Lewis states "it is quite true that if we took Christ's advice, we should soon be living in a happier world."[106]

Daily Bible Reading

---

[106] C.S. Lewis *Mere Christianity* (San Francisco: Harper Collins, 1952), 155.

First, we need to read and study God's Word (the Bible) every day. This is how you will learn about God's ways and how to overcome your problems and troubles. Just as one may set aside time to do other things in their lives; they should also schedule time to spend reading the Bible. The word of God brings strength to your spiritual nature. If you do not have a Bible, make your first prayer request to God to supply you with one.

This is one thing that is taken very seriously. There may have been times when one convinced himself that they didn't have time to read the Bible on a daily basis. They had every excuse in the world as to why they didn't. But like most people, some had to experience some type of tribulation before they would pick up a Bible. And again, like most folks, after they'd gotten through that specific circumstance, they would put the Bible on the back burner. This could go on for a long period of time or until one is enlightened.

"When you proceed to fight in your deliverance….then the spirit of God will take over and destroy demonic elements in the realm of the spirit."[107] Sometimes, we find ourselves fighting to do the right things but are met with negative spirits. This is the time to spend reading the Word of God. The Bible is one book that has all of the answers. This is when God will step in and take control. All one has to do is allow Him to do His work.

---

[107] Juanita Bynum *No More Sheets*. (Lanham, MD: Pneuma Life Publishing, 1998), 166.

One day while the "mother of the church" was sitting in her favorite chair reading her Bible, she was asked why she did this, and she proceeded to say that if it weren't for this good book, there is no telling where she would be. For the next couple hours, she opened up, speaking about some of her past experiences, the good and the bad, things that were unknown. But what was surprising was that for every experience she had, she could also point out a scripture or a story from the Bible. It was then that she said that no matter where you go in life, no matter what questions you had or what answers needed, they could be found right here in the Bible. At that moment, the choice had been made. From that day forth, every morning, a ritual was begun by getting up, get a cup of coffee, and spend the next twenty to thirty minutes reading the Bible. And most importantly, because one took time to study His word, a person could actually feel Him working in them and guiding their footsteps as they walked closer and closer to Him.

"Study to show thyself approved unto God, a workman that needeth not to be ashamed, rightly dividing the word of truth." (2Timothy 2:15 KJV) What this scripture is relaying is that if one would stay connected to the Word of God, it will enable them to better prepare for any adversity that may arise in their lives. "But thou hast fully known my doctrine, manner of life, purpose, faith, longsuffering, charity, patience, persecutions, afflictions, which came unto me at Antioch, at Iconium, at Lystra; what persecutions I endured: but out of them all the Lord delivered me. Yea, and all that will live godly in Christ Jesus shall suffer persecution. But evil men and seducers shall wax worse and worse, deceiving, and being deceived. But continue thou in the things which thou hast learned and hast been assured of, knowing of whom thou hast learned them; And that from a child thou hast known the Holy Scriptures, which are able to make thee wise unto salvation through faith which is in Christ Jesus. All scripture is given by inspiration of God, and is profitable for doctrine, for reproof, for correction, for instruction in righteousness: That the man of God may be perfect, thoroughly furnished unto all good works." (2Timothy 3:10 KJV)

However, if we look to God for direction, He will correct us, and He will instruct us to work hard and study all that is needed in order to bring a strong presence of healing the pain. When we allow God to correct us, he will become our friend. "God is able to repair the broken places, but it requires us to expose where those broken places are."[108] After you allow God to have His way in your life, your life will change. You begin to work on the closeness in Jesus. You make a choice not to worry, but to cast your worries on God.

Pray to God Every Day

We know that we have to seek God to get past the pains our lives. This can no way be accomplished if you choose to leave God out. The model used at CHMCLACC has no choice in the matter. God is sought in all that is done in this organization. The ingredients that he has blended together to make a more perfect work force. The knowledge gleaned from the accomplishments of a Psychologist who holds an M.B.A., J.D., Psy.D., D.MIN., among other degrees, gives clients chance to meet with professionals who are top in their fields. The twenty years it took to build this organization did not come easy. There was much pain and disappointments and distraction over the years. However; the lesson learned was life changes continuously and one must realize that sometimes it doesn't go as planned. But if you keep the faith, you will be productive to God's kingdom.

---

[108] T.D. Jakes. *Naked and Not Ashamed: We've Been Afraid to Reveal What God Longs to Heal.* (NY: Destiny Image Publishers, 1995), 9.

We must fellowship and talk to God if we are to hear His guidance and learn of His nature. We are promised that all of our needs shall be met if we will only ask the Father in the name of Jesus. Too many times, people think that it's hard to pray or that they don't know how to pray. But praying is just like hoping. I've mentioned to the younger generation that just as they may be in the middle of taking a test, they will hope to do well. Prayer is pretty much the same thing. Take time to have a conversation with God. Tell Him what's in your heart and what's on your mind.

According to Piper, "the return of prayer at the beginning of the twenty-first century is a remarkable work of God."[109] Most people don't realize just how powerful prayer is. When one takes their burdens to God, a load has been lifted.

---

[109] John Piper. *Let the Nations Be Glad! The Supremacy of God in Missions.*)Grand Rapids, MI: Baker Academic, 1993), 67.

No prayer ever goes unanswered. This is one thing that we can be certain of. On the other hand, sometimes, we are not happy with the answer that we received. Sometimes, we may not even recognize it as the answer because we are expecting something different. It takes willingness on our part to be free to accept whatever answers that are offered. There are times that our answers come unexpectedly; a chance meeting on the street, a nagging feeling within or even a passage from a newspaper or book. The one that that is certain is that God speaks to us throughout the day. Our prayers are answered, our worries are eased and problems find solutions, but only when we attune ourselves to the message. "You must first begin a relationship with God."[110] This is such an easy thing to do. All one has to do is to make the decision to follow God's instructions. Ms. Adamson goes on to give this example: "Imagine some guy named Mike decides to ask the president of Princeton University (whom Mike doesn't even know) to co-sign a car loan for him. Mike would have zero chance of that happening. (We're assuming that the president of Princeton is not an idiot.) However, if that same president's daughter asked her dad to co-sign a car loan for her, it would be no problem. Relationship matters."[111]

---

[110] Marilyn Adamson, "Does God Answers Our Prayers?" http://www.everystudent.com/wires/prayers.html; 26 November 2009.
[111] Ibid

With God, when the person is actually a child of God, when the person belongs to God, he knows them and hears their prayers. Jesus said, "I am the good shepherd. I know my sheep and my sheep know me . . . my sheep listen to my voice. I know them and they follow me. I give them eternal life and they shall never perish; no one can snatch them out of my hand." (John 10:14 NKJV)

When you're in a broken place, it is not the end of your story."[112] This statement is very true. God wants His children to come to him in their brokenness. He wants them to come to Him first. Sometimes, clients will use the excuse "I want to have my life together first." This is not what God wants. He knows that we all fall short and it's in these times that we should lean on Him the most. It's because of His grace and mercy that allows one to overcome any situation they may face. "Do what you can to move beyond problems that are related to your old way of thinking."[113] This can be done by disassociating yourself from those from the past. Sadly, family member can also be included in this group.

---

[112] Robert Schuller with William Kruidenier. *Leaning Into God when Life is Pushing You Away.* (NY: FaithWords, 2009), 86.

[113] Wayne Dyer *Excuses Begone! How to Change Lifelong, Self-Defeating Thinking Habits* (NY: Hay House Inc., 2009), 148.

Bob Phillips points out that "mental, emotional and spiritual growth comes from facing problems rather than running from them....one must be determined not to give up and accept responsibility for their actions."[114] It's hard and clients are made aware of this. Nothing is easily gained without putting in the work. If clients give up or give in, they are left feeling the same way as they did before they sought help. Encouraging them to move on, even when they feel defeated, is important to the staff at CHMCLACC. There comes a time when clients must be pushed in the direction in which they need to go in order to overcome painful situations.

However, if a person is gung-ho about reaching and achieving their goal, they will put everything they have within themselves to get to the other side. But "avoiding is much like denial in the sense that the person lies to themselves to avoid painful feelings."[115]

---

[114] Bob Phillips *Controlling Your Emotions Before They Control You* (Eugene, OR: Harvest House Publishers, 1995), 31.

[115] Joshua Coleman, *When Parents Hurt: Compassionate Strategies When You and Your Grown Child Don't Get Along* (NY: Harper Collins Publishers, 2007), 87.

There was a time when someone asked how often should they pray? When they were told that they should pray all day, every day, they were a bit surprised. But also found they were not only praying for themselves, but most importantly, the majority of their prayers were for someone else. They were informed that there are times when they may see a story on the news or in the newspaper, and the first thing they do is to pray for that person or family. It was relayed to him that just because you don't know someone, prayer is the best thing that we can give someone.

Too many times, people will react when they should have acted. Unfortunately, when experiencing painful situations, one would normally react to that situation. People have to want and learn to accept that this is a point in their lives where they must make changes. Change belongs to them, if they want it. A frown from a friend or spouse does not need to make one feel rejected. Criticism does not have to ruin one's day. Being in command of your own feelings and your own actions prevents that free-floating anxiety from grasping and putting a hold on them.

"If you let go of what's in your hand, God will let go of what's in His hand for you – peace, strength, wisdom."[116] Too many times, clients try to hold on to the old. This is the time to let all of that old stuff go and be open to receive what God has for them. Sadly, most people are afraid of the unknown and no matter how uncomfortable their present situation may be, they tend to hold on to it because it's something that they know or have become somewhat comfortable or content with. But if the client would just let all of that go and wait on God, he will be able to see the wondrous works of God.

As C.S. Lewis said in *Faith*, "The more God loves you, the more determined He must be to pull you back from your way into His way."[117] God does not want to see His children suffer and does everything in His power to rescue them from their negative situations. However, there will be times when the suffering itself is the lesson that they must go through in order to get them closer to God. This can be done when "people have a positive outlook generally report a better quality of spiritual life...a greater peace of mind."[118] By looking at what's positive in their surroundings, clients are given a better understanding of what they may be able to change in their own lives.

---

[116] Victoria Osteen, *Love Your Life, Living Happy, Healthy & Whole*. (NY: Free Press, 2008), 72.

[117] C.S. Lewis. *Faith*, (Nashville, TN: Thomas Nelson Inc., 1998), 45.

[118] Dan Baker, Cathy Greenberg, Ina Yalof *What Happy Women Know: How New Findings in Positive Psychology Can Change Womens' Lives for the Better* (NY:Rodale, 2007), 183.

Clients at CHMCLACC learn that through "weakened faith in the future leads to anxiety and depression, which disrupts thought process."[119] While working through their issues, clients must realize that they should not fear what the future may hold but trust in God's plan for their lives and work diligently to continue on that path. Just as David Jeremiah pointed out in Living With Confidence, "No matter what we face, the abounding love and compassion of God are more than sufficient..."[120] Everyone will face a difficult time in their lives. But if they put their trust in God's Word, they will get through. It may be a rough road ahead, there may be some tears cried, but through it all, God is with them. They, the clients, just need to wait on God's will and be patient and know that He is already working it out. Even when they may not see what's happening, God is in control.

    The negativity of pain only breeds more negativity. "Negative emotions arise from past associations that repeat themselves."[121] Fortunately, its opposite does likewise. One's attitude will carry them a long way, and a positive attitude will make all things possible. People are meant for good living—not for living a life full of pain. But one must seek it out and be open to its invitation. And having faith in their ability to overcome their pain and achieve their dreams will make it easier to take the necessary steps.

---

[119] B.F. Skinner *About Behaviorism* (NY: Alfred Knopf, 1974), 154.

[120] David Jeremiah *Living with Confidence in a Chaotic World: What on Earth Should We Do?* (TN: Thomas Nelson Publishing, 1999), 28.

[121] Joan Borysenko. *Minding the Body, Mending the Mind* (NY: Bantam Books, 1987), 115.

In David Edwards' Worship 365, he touches on how a person must seek out God in prayer in order to overcome painful situations. James 4:8 reads "Draw near to God, and He will draw near to you. Cleanse your hands, sinners, and purify your hearts, double-minded people."[122] This quote should make clients aware that they have to cleanse themselves of the old ways and be open to receive God's word. If he continues to go to God with a closed heart, it will not allow him to receive the blessing that God has for him.

According to Piper, "the return of prayer at the beginning of the twenty-first century is a remarkable work of God."[123] Most people don't realize just how powerful prayer is. Clients at CHMCLACC are instructed to take their burdens to God and once this is done, the load has been lifted.

---

[122] David Edwards, *Worship 365: The Power of a Worshiping Life* (Nashville, TN: Broadman & Holman Publishers, 2006), 37.

[123] John Piper. *Let the Nations Be Glad! The Supremacy of God in Missions.* (Grand Rapids, MI: Baker Academic, 1993), 67.

There was a father having a conversation with his son, who once said that he didn't know how to pray. His father told him that prayer is really having a conversation with God. But before you do this, you must be open to receive what God has to say. Just take the time to, first, thank God for allowing you to be the person you are. He questioned why people would continue to pray when there is so much suffering going on in the world. His father told him that first and foremost, most of the suffering, violence, hurt, abuse, and so on is caused by humans. God gives everyone us free will, and it's up to everyone to take that free will and do what's right. However, there is always someone who will also choose to do the total opposite. When God says to go left, they'll go right. It's a choice that they've made. But, when you take the time to get to know God, to study His word, this is when He shows up.

The entire Bible is a description of the kind of relationship God wants us to experience with Him and the kind of life He wants to give us. From the very beginning, God has a plan for everyone's life. God only wants the best for His children. However, there are rules and instructions that He wants us to follow. "The Lord delights in those who fear [reverence] Him, who put their hope in His unfailing love." (Psalm 147:10-11 NIV)

However, God's greatest display of his love and commitment to you is this: Jesus said, "Greater love hath no man than this, that a man lay down his life for his friends," (John 15:13 KJV), which is what Jesus did for us. "When character is not in place, God works on the heart."[124] This is according to Henry Blackaby. God looks at the inside of His children instead of the outside. He looks at the heart and not the mind.

It's a feeling that's hard to describe, but as the old folks have said, "when you know that you know that you know," the feeling of His power is something that comes from within. Dr. Towns states that "worship is an experience and there are six elements that should happen in all true worship: examination, expectation, appropriate, meditation, consummation and transformation."[125] It's something that touches the very depths of your soul and your heart. "And whatsoever ye shall ask in my name, that will I do, that the Father may be glorified in the Son. If ye shall ask any thing in my name, I will do it. If ye love me, keep my commandments." (John 14:13-14 KJV). As the scripture reads, "Seek ye first the kingdom of God, and his righteousness; and all these things shall be added unto you" (Matt. 6:33).

Sharing Beliefs With Like-minded People

---

[124] Henry Blackaby *Created to be God's Friend* (Nashville, TN: Thomas Nelson Publishers, 1999), 148.

[125] Elmer Towns, *Perimeter of Light: Biblical Boundaries for the Emerging Church* (Chicago: Moody Publishers, 2004). 85.

Christian fellowship occurs when two or more Christians are in one another's company. The dictionary defines fellowship as "friendly association with others; companionship." Christian fellowship, then, involves friendly association with other Christians which means you should choose Christians to be your companions. When a person fellowships with others sharing their same religious beliefs, they will "strengthen their relationships and appreciation for each other and create unity."[126]

Ask the Lord to show you the people you are to pray and fellowship with. He does not want you to be alone in your Christian walk. We need one another's prayers, encouragement, and love to grow in God. Try to meet others who share in your religious beliefs. By having someone who is working towards the same goal will make your Christian walk a whole lot easier and enjoyable. "And let us consider one another to provoke unto love and to good works: Not forsaking the assembling of ourselves together, as the manner of some is; but exhorting one another: and so much the more, as ye see the day approaching" (Hebrews 10:24-25 KJV)

---

[126] Glen Martin and Gary McIntosh. *The Issachar Factor: Understanding Trends that Confront Your Church and Designing a Strategy for Success.* Nashville, TN. Broadman & Holman Publishers. 1993. 32.

David Jeremiah stated that "in order to keep your heart pure, you must have the wisdom of God."[127] Until a person can open their heart fully to God's wisdom, it cannot truly be pure to receive God's blessings. Job 28:1-11 states "Job began to use several illustrations of things that are sought after. Silver is mined from deep in the Earth and gold is refined and separated from the rock in which it is embedded (Verse 1). Iron is taken from the earth by great effort, and copper is melted from the one in which it is resides (V2). Man digs deep into the earth and goes where no man has ever gone before to find treasure (V3). But one cannot find the treasure of wisdom this way. Man cannot find God's wisdom by mere human efforts. This search takes more than courage and native intelligence. It demands humility and spiritual perception."[128]

The Book of Church Growth shows us a way to fellowship with those sharing the same beliefs. During meetings of small groups, "each attendee is asked to keep a vacant chair next to them, giving them the responsibility of bringing others to the group."[129] Clients at CHMCLACC are required to attend group meetings to exchange thoughts, prayers, personal stories, etc. By doing this, it allows them to share their experiences with God in a church-like community and according to Robert Dale, this is when "a congregational body of belief emerges."[130]

[127] David Jeremiah. *Tried, Tested and Triumphant: The Book of Job.* Vols. 1 & 2. San Diego, CA. Self-published. 2010. 50-51.

[128] ____. Ibid, 51.

[129] Larry Crabb. *It's Time to Connect.* 246.

Christian fellowship begins through a process of adoption. Are you a Christian today? If you are, you have been adopted by God. You may have heard it said that we are all God's children, but the truth is, we don't become God's children until we are adopted, through faith in Christ. God predestined us to be adopted as his sons through Jesus Christ, in accordance with his pleasure and will.

If we were all God's children by virtue of being His creation, then adoption wouldn't be necessary. Ask any parents of adopted children, and they'll tell you the process is long, hard, and painful! Why would God choose adoption if we were already His children? Because God longs to have you as His child, He sacrificed Himself, in the person of Jesus Christ, on the cross in order to purchase your salvation. So if you've received Christ as your personal Savior and Lord, congratulations! You are now a member of God's family.

Keep Your Heart Pure

Ask God to cleanse you of all sin and impure thoughts and motives. Satan, our enemy, will try to break our fellowship with God by getting us back into sin or trying to get us angry at God. One way to guard against these feelings is to resist the devil daily.

When we go to God in prayer, we must make sure that our hearts are filled with love. We can't go to Him with hatred for others. We must open our hearts and minds to receive what He has for us, even when we may think otherwise. How many times have we decided that we are going to help God help us? I find this to be hilarious. And when we make decisions such as this, most of the time, we get in the way of our own blessings. It's hard sometimes to sit back and feel as though you're not doing anything, but sometimes, this is exactly what God wants us to do. We should submit ourselves to Him fully. "Submit yourselves therefore to God. Resist the devil and he will flee from you." (James 4:7 KJV)

A.W. Tozer wrote, "Left to ourselves, we tend to immediately reduce God to manageable terms. We want to get Him where we can use Him or at least, know where He is when we need Him, we want a God we can in some measure, control."[131] We support this with the book of Isaiah. God has chosen to speak in this manner "For my thoughts are not your thoughts, nor are your ways my ways," says the Lord. "For as the heavens are higher than the earth, so are my ways higher than your ways and my thoughts, your thoughts." Isaiah 55:8-9.

---

[131] A.W. Tozer, *The Knowledge of the Holy: The Attitudes of God: There Meaning in the Christian Life.* (New York: Harper San Francisco, 1992). 8.

If you have a sound and spiritual attitude in your relationship with God, you will keep God first in your mind, asking yourself along the way: "am I in God's will when I move. Do I show love in what I do?"[132] Yes. This has to be a requirement in keeping your relationship with God. "If we think we can measure God like that, we are going to miss the beauty of our creator. He is so overwhelmingly amazing that sometimes, all we can do is bow down before Him and worship."[133]

Let Jesus Avenge

During the course of life, everyone has experienced painful and hurtful situations. Oftentimes, we go through a period where we feel the need to "get back" at the person or persons that have caused us this pain. However, the Bible states, "Vengeance is mine, saith the Lord." (Romans 12:19 KJV)

There are plenty of things that one can do to get over this feeling to hurt the one that has hurt us. Most importantly, we must turn to the Scriptures. Also, when we do take things into our own hands, it seems to make the situation a whole lot worse. By taking the time to think about the consequences of what our actions can lead to, it will give us the time to cool off and let God handle the situation.

---

[132] Ibid., FF

[133] Ibid., 48.

If we take the time to listen, Jesus speaks to us just as he spoke to Paul saying "My Grace is sufficient for thee, for my strength is made perfect in weakness." (2Cor. 12:9 KJV) According to David Edwards' Worship 365, what Jesus is saying today is, "Live in Me, walk in Me, follow Me, acknowledge Me in all your ways."[134] It is not a good idea to seek revenge when someone does something a person may not like. Of course it may hurt and make a person angry, but if they take matters into their own hands, it only adds to their current situation. They've allowed someone else to make them act out in a way that is not pleasing to God. As Laura Schlessinger states "don't let revenge cast a shadow on your soul and very being."[135]

Approximately twenty years ago, a friend of mine had gone through a devastating situation regarding the infidelity of his wife. When he came to me, he was very upset and angry. At the time, all he wanted to do was to hurt his wife the way that she had hurt him. He came up with plenty of ideas. However, I told him that this was not the way to go. I understood his hurt and his anger and told him that if he didn't let this situation handle itself, he would be the one to end up paying.

---

[134] David Edwards. *Worship 365: The Power of a Worshiping Life*. (Nashville, TN. Broadman & Holman Publishers. 2006), 43.

[135] Laura Schlessinger *Surviving a Shark Attack (On Land): Overcoming Betrayals and Dealing with Revenge* (NY: Harper Collins Publishers, 2011), 117.

Well, approximately one week later, he just happened upon the man who had been involved with his wife. The first thing he did was to approach this man, a few words were exchanged, and before you knew it, this gentleman friend had assaulted this man. Once the police were called, the aggressor friend was arrested and charged with assault. He spent three days in jail before he was able to make bail.

After making bail, he decided that in order for him to make the necessary changes in his life, he would need help. And the help he needed could only come from having a relationship with Jesus. Although it was very tough for him to give up his way of life, he knew that if he didn't put the effort into having a relationship with Jesus, he wouldn't have much of a life anyway. He was so worried about how it would make him look in the eyes of those that he used to hang around with. But as we know, God has power to show you just who God is. And when this gentleman finally received Jesus as his savior, it no longer mattered what others thought of him.

Today, not only is he a deacon in his church but he also has a ministry of his own. He now goes out into the very same neighborhoods that he menaced to reach out to the younger generation in hopes of steering them in the right direction, just as Jesus has steered him on his Christian walk. At the beginning, he was met with doubt and reservation, which was very upsetting to him. But he made a promise to God that he would push forward; and push forward he did. With money that he'd made over the course of his previous life, he not only donated much to the church but he also took that money and put it back into the community.

What started off as him wanting to help the young generation to stay in school and, more importantly, to have a relationship with Jesus, he became a great outlet to many of the single mothers of boys. He became a "counselor" of sorts and would sit down with them as well to help them help their children. What he didn't realize is that the more he made his presence in the community for doing good, the more people he brought to church, and in turn more and more of these folks began their own relationship with Jesus.

Let Jesus Be Your Peace of Mind

Absent of the calming peace of Jesus' presence, many have turned to artificial means of comfort. Alternatives such as drugs, alcohol, fornication, adultery, homosexuality, education, business, politics, material possessions, sports, bar hopping, or just anything but Jesus. The trouble with these alternatives is that they don't work. They are temporary solutions to permanent and recurring issues in our everyday lives. Unfortunately, when someone is experiencing a painful situation, suicide becomes the predictable choice that many turn to when the resolution is not found in the alternative that they have turned to. It doesn't have to be that way.

In *Church Without Walls*, Jim Peterson tells us that "the journey to Christ is not just an event, but a process and that one of the most common mistakes made is trying to do it all at once."[136] The entire process takes time, but it's time well spent when clients are investing in making their lives better.

"Modern medicine can heal afflictions of the body, but only God can heal the mind."[137] Bishop Jakes' quote is another important aspect that a client must realize. Although there have been plenty of prescriptions given to clients to combat emotional problems, the bottom line is that God can control the mind and make the necessary changes in order for a person to move past the old and into the new.

---

[136] Jim Peterson. *Church Without Walls*.)Colorado Springs, CO. NavPress. 1992), 190.

[137] T.D. Jakes. *It's Time to Reveal What God Longs to Heal*. (PA. Destiny Image Publishers, 1995), 36.

Pain has a way of stretching us. It pushes us toward others and encourages us to pray. We also develop our character while handling painful times. Pain prepares us to help others whose experiences are the same as ours. When we reflect on our past, we can remember the pain we felt last month or even last year; the pain of no job and bills, the pain of losing a loved one or children leaving home. At the time, it may seem that we couldn't cope, but somehow we did, and it felt good. What we must not forget is that we never have to experience pain alone.

Paul in his letter to the people of Corinth said that what Moses and his people went through in the desert should serve as a warning to us; it should be a reminder of those things that the Lord was not pleased with. The good news for us is that God through his son can give us a permanent peace of mind. Yes, we will have temptation but, as Paul comforts the Corinthians: "No temptation has seized you except what is common to man. And God is faithful; he will not let you be tempted beyond what you can bear. But when you are tempted, he will also provide a way out so that you can stand up under it" (1Corinthians 10:13 NKJV)

In MLK Jr. Is the Dream Still Alive," Dr. Willie Mason states that "until spiritual change takes place, social political and economical changes will not last."[138] It is very human to worry. So, it is humanly natural for us to cling to our worries, to the point that we become fearful, which sends us into desperation. I am reminded of a spiritual, "What a Friend We Have in Jesus," that says, "What a friend we have in Jesus, all our sins and grief we bear;" yet, how quickly we turn to what is natural. There is nothing in our lives that we can control without giving over our lives to God. Solomon, full of God's wisdom, faced his limitation. In *Keeping Company With Jesus*, Jackie Smallbones states: "There comes a time for each of us to spend time alone with God to hear him address us personally."[139]

One instance that I am reminded of is when a very good friend of mine found out that she was unable to have children. This woman was the type that loved all children. She spent many hours taking care of the children of relatives and friends and couldn't wait to become a mother to her own child. However, due to health reasons, she was unable to bear children. For the first couple of years after receiving this news, she was very, very bitter. She continued to question herself as well as God. There was a time when she asked, "Why me?"

---

[138] Willie Mason. *Martin Luther King Jr. Is the Dream Still Alive?* (Bloomington, IN: Author House, 2006), 110.

[139] Jackie Smallbones. *Keeping Company with Jesus: Reflections on Gospel Stories.* (Minneapolis: Augsburg Books, 2005), 87.

For a while, she was very angry. She felt that there were so many women giving birth to babies but were not capable of providing for them. Even worse, she had witnessed some mothers having child after and child and allowing family members to take care of their children as they went on with their lives. She found herself getting more and more upset at what she thought was unfair. Why would God allow these types of women to keep giving birth to babies that they really didn't want? Why would God take that most precious experience away from her, someone who would give anything to have a child of her own?

Finally, about four years after she accepted her situation, she prayed to God for answers. And the answer she received was that all children belonged to her. It was at this moment that she began to feel a peace that she'd never felt before. "The person who readily overcomes adversity exercises the self-discipline to think positively."[140] From this day on, she took the time to spend with children who were at risk of not receiving the proper care. She purchased books, toys, and clothes and would take them to families in need. This was the beginning of a great ministry. It was then that she thanked God for giving her the opportunity to mother many, many children, and she took great pride in being there for these children. As the scripture reads: "Trust in the Lord with all thine heart and lean not on thine own understanding, in all thy ways acknowledge him, and he shall direct thy." (Proverbs 3:5-6 KJV).

---

[140] Andrew DuBrin *Getting it Done: The Transforming Power of Self-Discipline* (NJ: Peterson's/Pacesetter Books, 1995), 189.

"Scriptures declare that heroes were made strong out of weakness."[141] When a client comes into the center, he is usually at his lowest in life and thinking that there is nothing that can be done. But God has used the least of the least and made them the best of the best. Trust is all that He wants His children to do. Trust that He will make a way out of no way. He can turn the weakest man into the strongest.

If clients take the time to listen, Jesus speaks to his brethren just as he spoke to Paul saying "My Grace is sufficient for you, for power is perfected in weakness." (2Cor. 12:9 NKJV). According to David Edwards' Worship 365, what Jesus is saying today is "Life in Me, walk in Me, follow Me, acknowledge Me in all your ways."[142]

It is almost impossible to avoid some sort of pain. Just about everyone has some sort of pain and many find it hard to survive. Thankfully, some will seek out assistance in relieving them of their problems whether through counseling, self-help books, etc.

Clients at CHMCLACC will learn that pain, no matter how uncomfortable, prepares us to better serve God, as well as others. There are times when one may hold on to that pain because he fear what he may have to deal with on the other side of that pain. Sadly, some people will allow themselves to be controlled by not knowing instead of putting their trust in God.

---

[141] T.D. Jakes. *It's Time to Reveal What God Longs to Heal*. (PA. Destiny Image Publishers. 1995), 36.

[142] David Edwards. *Worship 365: The Power of a Worshiping Life* (Nashville, TN: Broadman & Holman Publishers, 2006), 43.

"The Holy Spirit is calling for the broken, infirm people to come to Jesus. He will restore and deliver."[143] Again, God wants His children to come to Him when they are at their worst. He does not want them to wait until they can no longer handle their problems themselves. He is there for all of His children, 24/7. All one has to do is cry out to Him and He will hear their cries.

In order to obtain that peace of mind through Jesus, we must first surrender to a power greater than ourselves. With each day, we have to turn to Jesus for strength and guidance. We must learn and accept that we cannot control forces outside of ourselves. We cannot control the actions of our family or coworkers. However, we can control our responses to them. And when we choose to surrender our attempts to control, we will find peace and serenity. While working on achieving a peace of mind, clients are reminded that Paul "tells us to pray for peace because of God's desire that all be saved and come to know the truth."[144]

---

[143] T.D. Jakes. *Power for Living*. (PA. Destiny Image Publishers. 1995), 128.

[144] John Piper. *Let the Nations Be Glad! The Supremacy of God in Missions*. (Grand Rapids, MI: Baker Academic, 1993), 50.

The realities in life normally come to us in mysterious ways. We fight hard, only to realize that what we need will never be ours until the struggle is forsaken. Surrendering to Jesus brings enlightenment into our lives. As we stand before any problems or unfamiliar events, we may be overwhelmed with the feeling of dread. But the choice available to us now and always is to invite the spirit of Jesus into the space we're in. Our lives will be eased in proportion to our faith that God is there, caring for our every concern, putting before us what we need to grow. We will be able to let go of our doubts, pains and anguish.

It is at this stage, that God wants us to trust in Him. One must rely on their faith in God to get through the tough times in their lives. God asks us to trust his integrity, his character, his compassion, love, wisdom, righteousness on our behalf. He says, "I have loved you with an everlasting love, therefore I have continued my faithfulness to you." (Jeremiah 31:1 KJV). "Trust in him at all times, O people. Pour out your heart before him."(Psalm 62:8 KJV). God wants his children to bring their burden to Him and He will guide us. "God is a refuge for us." (Psalm 46:1 KJV).

Dr. Jamal Bryant wrote "The emotional pressures you sense often from people you've known for a long time tries to push you in a particular direction."[145] If you take a moment and think about what is really happening, you'll see the pressure you feel, which your mind might interpret as pain, is trying to divert you away from a solution to your situation; from facing an issue you've avoided for a long time, or from inner struggles you don't want to address. He goes on to say that "That pressure makes you want to run and hide. Hide in drugs, a spending spree or an eating binge. You may even want to bury your head in the sand and ignore the problem and the treatment one more time. You've got to fight against the pressure."[146]

The depths of your pain or fear should not hold you in a place of progressive pain, but an outlet to minimize the pain. If the pain is not addressed or attended to, it will intensify its need of resolve.

"We understand that I am the weapon of God,"[147] Dr. Bryant wrote in *World War Me*. He further supports this with Jeremiah 51:20-21 which reads: "You are my war club, my weapon for battle – with you I destroy kingdoms, with you I shatter chariot and driver..." Dr. Bryant goes on to say "your gift and that special ability and calling you received from God was given to you for the purpose of blessing the people around you. Joseph didn't realize it, but at the very moment he became a powerful tool. He became a weapon in God's hand."[148]

---

[145] Jamal Bryant, *World War Me*. (Baltimore: Empowerment, 2009), 119.

[146] Ibid., 120

Secondly, Dr. Bryant states that "there is no greater pain of being hurt by your own family, a family that can't see your gift and doesn't like your dream. They don't realize you are called out, separated and different from everyone else. Joseph's own family attacked him and threw him in a pit."[149]

Pain is here. The different circumstances that an individual may encounter has much to do with how they will respond and treat people who may be in a similar situation. We wonder how this is. We know that the present situation has no impact on how God carries you through the process of your pain. You will have some count on it. The process of pain is seen throughout the word of God as the thing that will change your life...one way or another.

Chapter Five
Research/Case Study

---

[147] Ibid., 156

[148] Ibid., 156

[149] Ibid., 158

In Conclusion, we will take a deeper look at Choosing Hope Ministries' Christian Legal Aid and Clinical Counseling Center. This center came to fruition in 2001 as an outreach ministry by Rev. Dr. Ronnie Moore. From a very early age, Dr. Moore was always involved in helping others. Raised by his grandparents, he started working in the church at the age of 7. By the time he reached the age of 12, he was elected to the position of Jr. Superintendant of the Sunday school, where over the years; he has held many different positions.

In 2000, the decision was made to start this ministry to help those less fortunate. At the very beginning of the organization, there were only two people who were a part of this organization and between those two individuals; the organization eventually grew to include professionals specializing in various degrees.

Dr. Moore's decision to bring in these professionals was considered "outside of the box," but this is what makes CHMCLACC so successful in their counseling center. Being that clients come in with a myriad of problems, having professionals on staff makes the counseling sessions a greater success because the client can address not only their emotional issues, but as well as other issues that most likely, is the cause of their distress.

CHMCLACC has been solely financed by God and Dr. Moore, whether it is assisting a household with groceries, helping with utility bills, prescriptions, etc. One specific case comes to mind is the case of the single mother who had a sick child. This child required monthly visits to a hospital out of state and the vehicle she had at the time was in dire need of repair. This was a concern for Dr. Moore because he knew how important it was for this child to receive his treatments and was concerned that the state of the vehicle would prevent him from making all of his appointments. Dr. Moore used his 15-plus years of experience in car sales and took her to purchase a new vehicle. Not only did he work out an acceptable deal for her, for the first two years, he committed to paying a portion of her car payment, which allowed her to become financially stable.

Over the years, CHMCLACC has donated much to those less fortunate in the communities. Every Christmas, through donations from friends and family, the center would donate toys to families in need. The majority of these families may not have come through the center, but the center was informed that they were in need. This is where CHMCLACC's motto began, "Meeting People at Their Needs."

CHMCLACC also has a book drive periodically where books are donated to those in the community, especially the children. Education is greatly stressed at the center and Dr. Moore tries to make it as fun as possible for the children, but most importantly, he wants to make it accessible.

Choosing Hope Ministries Christian Legal Aid and Clinical Counseling

(CHMCLACC) has used in counseling clients through difficult and painful situations. Along with using Creation Therapy, which deals with the temperaments, the Center also focuses on educating the client on the underlying reason(s) that caused them to feel depressed, stressed, or overwhelmed. We will look at five interviews that have come through the Center.

Suing the Law School

Preface: *The names are withheld due to mutual agreement and confidentiality laws.*

Q: What brought you to the center?

A: I entered into a law school three years ago. In my last year of attending, I experienced financial hardship. Although I had was going through this hardship, I was able to complete my studies, along with submission of a dissertation, which I received the grade of "A" and graduated with a GPA of 3.5. Because of the hardship, I went to the school and proposed a payment plan, which would have allowed me to receive my degree. The payment plan that was submitted was never responded to. Along with other financial burdens, I was left with no other choice than to file a chapter 7 bankruptcy.

In the process of filing this bankruptcy, I had an option to have a payment plan approved by the bankruptcy court. That plan was submitted to be approved by the court. It was never returned from the law school. With all of the unnecessary stress and pain and having gone this far, and at the end, I would have hoped that a school that I had worked so hard in, would work with me to finalize my law school education. But they chose to threaten me through email communication that I would not receive my law degree, that they would not submit my records, they would not validate my attendance at the school if I did not comply with their demands.

However, I continued to pursue resolution through the school by providing a document that would need their signature and calculations for approval of the court. Again, the school chose to ignore my request. Nonetheless, because of the email communications was in violation of Bankruptcy Code 11"USC 362 (A)(6) disallowing them the right to pursue any collection activity or contact of debt."[150]

Q: What was your emotional state of mind at that time?

---

[150] Alan N. Resnick, Henry J. Sommer, *2011 Bankruptcy Code: Bankruptcy Code, As Amended, And Related Statutory Provisions Pt. 1* (CA: Matthew Bender & Company, 2010), 236. Any act to collect, access, or recover a claim against the debtor that arose before the commence before the case under this title:

A: At that time I was hurt, disappointed, frustrated and being in an atmosphere of being totally mistreated. I wanted to get past this pain, but I also wanted to receive what I had worked so hard for. I was lead to believe by the school that because of my financial hardship, that I would be a complete failure and I would have no documentation of my three years of law school.

I needed something more than just a legal component and a psychological component. I needed a process that would allow me the opportunity to gain the understanding, understand the hurts and move past the pain.

Q: What was the process?

A: The process has been described in understanding your temperament, having a understanding of your pain, choosing to worship through your pain versus complain, pray for changes, make Jesus your best friend, read the Bible daily and pray to the Lord every day, learn to let Jesus avenge and e your peace of mind. And through this process, you will not only learn how to deal with pain, but that God can change anything through prayer according to His will, and you will inherit steps to move past the pain while God makes you over.

I have to be totally honest. At the beginning, I kept asking myself why should I have to go through so many steps and even more confusing was what did Jesus and praying have to do with a law suit? I even questioned the temperaments. But after submitting to the APS report and seeing the results, I was totally blown away. The results of the test were so close to who I was that it was almost scary. It was at this point where I figured I had nothing to lose.

During the course of my counseling sessions, I came to understand just how important God was in our everyday lives. I was raised going to church, but stepped away in my teen years. I was also a believer in God, but never took the time to get to know Him or His word. But after a few sessions and daily reading of the Bible, I came to a better understanding of not only myself, but God and Christianity. I was amazed that some of the people that God chose to be great leaders were indeed at one time, criminals, etc. I knew at this point that I too, could be successful.

One aspect I found interesting at CHM's center was they had more than just counselors on staff. I was able to speak to an attorney as well as a counselor. The attorney was able to address my questions regarding what legal action I could take in order to receive my degree. So, not only were my emotional state being addressed, I was also being taught about the legal process as well, which enabled me to make the right decisions pertaining to my law suit.

Although I was a bit standoffish at first, I am so very thankful that I was able to humble myself and allow the process to work

Q: What was the outcome?

A: The outcome resulted in the law school had thirty days to pay a sum of thousands of dollars or submit my degree to me. The degree was received within sixteen days of the court order.

Foreclosure I

Q: What brought you to the center?

A: I was told that I was unable to file a chapter 7 bankruptcy because my median income was over $75,000 which is what the federal government rates as median income. I was told by a friend of mine that an organization can help me to get to the root of this, but dealing with a previous law firm, in a year-long of objections and amendments, the plan was never confirmed along with that, there was an illegal sale of the residence in 2008. As of today, the property is still owned by me and no action is being pursued, thanks to CHM for retrieving forensic audit, securitization and title search, which gave me information to help me better prepare myself for the litigation I was up against. I was very discouraged with the law firm that I hired, failed to provide any of the information that CHM had provided to me. I was still convinced that the information that I received was valid. I sought the representation of another law firm, which pursued my initial thoughts.

Issues arose that allowed the attorney to change her initial perception. While still utilizing this attorney, I consulted with an organization that assured me that this could be done.

Q: What was your emotional state of mind at that time?

A: I was devastated and fearful of losing my home. I became quite depressed, angry and resentful. My family suffered a great deal because of my emotional state. I couldn't bring myself to take care of basic household needs.

Q: What was the process?

A: The process has been described in understanding your temperament, having a understanding of your pain, choosing to worship through your pain versus complain, pray for changes, make Jesus your best friend, read the Bible daily and pray to the Lord every day, learn to let Jesus avenge and e your peace of mind. And through this process, you will not only learn how to deal with pain, but that God can change anything through prayer according to His will, and you will inherit steps to move past the pain while God makes you over.

When I first saw the list of steps that I had to go through, I was kind of shocked. I'd spoken to friends who have gone through counseling and not one of them spoke of these types of steps. This in itself made me a little leery, but I had to understand that I had come to a Christian organization.

Not only did I learn a lot about myself during the temperament counseling, I came to an understanding of how and why I reacted the way I did. I was surprised at the outcome of the profile test because it was right on the mark. I have always been a believer but I wasn't a church goer. I'd go occasionally and on special holidays but that was just about it. However; after finishing my sessions, I became more involved in my walk with Christ and chose to find a church where I could continue fellowshipping with those who shared my Christian beliefs.

Knowing that God was still in control over this situation made it much easier to deal with. After realizing that all I had to do was trust in Him and His word, I made up my mind that no matter what was put in front of me, with God as my guide, I would prevail

Q: What was the outcome?

A: Four years later, the information that was shared with me, through Choosing Home Ministries' organization was valid, because the chapter 7 bankruptcy has been discharged.

Foreclosure II

Q: What brought you to the center?

A: Misrepresentation from a law firm and ill advice. A mortgage company chose to change the locks on the home while the home was under the 11USC362 Bankruptcy protection's Automatic Stay.

Q: What was your emotional state at the time?

A: Of course I was afraid, depressed and downright angry. All of my possessions were still inside of the residence and I had no way to retrieve them.

Q: What was the process?

A: The process has been described in understanding your temperament, having a understanding of your pain, choosing to worship through your pain versus complain, pray for changes, make Jesus your best friend, read the Bible daily and pray to the Lord every day, learn to let Jesus avenge and e your peace of mind. And through this process, you will not only learn how to deal with pain, but that God can change anything through prayer according to His will, and you will inherit steps to move past the pain while God makes you over

I'm going to be the first to admit that I wasn't trying to go through all of these steps. I figured talking to the counselor would be enough. How wrong was I? When I finally made up my mind to submit and follow the directions of CHM, I slowly began to feel like a weight was slowly being lifted off of me. I wasn't as angry or afraid because I knew that God was with me. Not being a reader, I slowly began reading my Bible. I'd make myself read a minimum of three Scriptures a day and before long, I found myself reading the Bible every day and to my surprise, I enjoyed it.

This has helped me to become a better person in general, but most importantly, I became a better Christian. Not only was my life a lot better, but because my attitude had been adjusted through counseling, the lives of those around me became better as well. I was a much happier person.

Q: What was the outcome?

A: Financial Settlement and renewing of the mortgage.

Bench Warrant

Q: What brought you to the center?

A: I was facing two counts of forgery and utterance for writing a bad check approximately a year prior. It was during the thanksgiving weekend and a warrant was issued for my arrest. My mother had me to contact CHM's organization who chose to assist me.

Q: What was the emotional state during that time?

A: I was an emotional wreck because at the time, I had two young babies at home and was afraid of having to be away from them or even worse, having them end up in the care of the state during the holiday weekend or me having to spend time in jail due to the holiday and no one being available for the bail.

Q: What was the process?

A: The process has been described in understanding your temperament, having a understanding of your pain, choosing to worship through your pain versus complain, pray for changes, make Jesus your best friend, read the Bible daily and pray to the Lord every day, learn to let Jesus avenge and e your peace of mind. And through this process, you will not only learn how to deal with pain, but that God can change anything through prayer according to His will, and you will inherit steps to move past the pain while God makes you over

During the course of working the steps, I began to get a better understanding of who I was. The temperament counseling session was an eye-opener for me. But learning the different personalities gave me a better insight on who I was. I came to realize that if I put in the effort to study my Bible, I'd be amazed of the stories that I could relate to. And to make it even more surprising, I was able to use the Bible in my everyday life.

I think the step that was most important to me there were attorneys on staff who could help me to understand the legal process I was facing and not only that, the attorney was right there with me in court. I also found I enjoyed being able to be around others who were going through similar situations. I didn't feel like I was the only one going through emotional problems.

I make it a point to read my bible every day. I learned through my sessions how important it is to spend some time reading God's word.

Q: What was the outcome?

A: The bench warrant that was ordered for my arrest, I was allowed to be brought to court by CHM before the judge removed the bench warrant and allowed me an opportunity to pay for the checks and once the checks were paid, the charges and conviction would be removed from my records. This is what CHM told me they would be able to get accomplished for me by following the steps of their program. Best of all, I was able to spend the holiday with my family.

Workers Compensation Case

Q: What brought you to the center?

A: I referred to the center by a mutual friend. I was going through a worker's compensation case and was told by three different law firms that my case was only worth no more than $20,000. However, I had close to $200,000 in medical bills alone as well as having gone through two surgeries.

Q: What was your emotional state of mind?

A: I was quite angry because these law firms were not honest with me. After contacting CHM, I found that my case was worth a lot more than what these firms had quoted to me. I was also fearful of not having enough finances to pay my monthly expenses. The insurance company only offered a settlement of $20,000. This settlement was seen by the commissioner as too low and was refused. It was during this time that I also suffered a heart attack, which brought on more burdens financially and emotionally.

I also felt that the law firms that I contacted were not looking out for my best interest. I found that the information I received from them was not true and also, I believe that I they didn't think it was worth their time or effort.

Q: What was the process?

A: The process has been described in understanding your temperament, having a understanding of your pain, choosing to worship through your pain versus complain, pray for changes, make Jesus your best friend, read the Bible daily and pray to the Lord every day, learn to let Jesus avenge and e your peace of mind. And through this process, you will not only learn how to deal with pain, but that God can change anything through prayer according to His will, and you will inherit steps to move past the pain while God makes you over.

I felt that the steps provided were the best thing to happen to me. I was so depressed when I first came to the center that I didn't know what I was going to do. But the model used at CHM is much more than what I've come across at other counseling centers. This is the only counseling center that I know of that has other professionals on staff. If someone in my predicament came in, they not only had access to the counselor, but they also had the opportunity to address any legal, real estate or business issue because the center offered these professionals as part of their model.

The one thing I liked was the use of God's word. Until I was able to give my burdens over, I felt bound. I had no peace. But the more and more I came to understand how important Jesus was in my life, the more peaceful I became. I learned to let go of the negative and hurtful feelings and concentrate on making Jesus my friend

Q: What was the outcome?

A: After gathering all of my medical records and information pertaining to the injury, CHM was able to negotiate a better deal which resulted in the insurance company being made to pay an additional $60,000 to me.

The one aspect of using this type of educational model is it gives the client the knowledge and explanations of the very thing or things that have caused them to experience the painful situations in the first place. As in the foreclosure case, client "A" was amazed at how little she knew of this process. Too many times, people will invest in something and not do the necessary research at the beginning of the process and not realize it until it's too late.

A little advice is to not to accept these truths on face value. Discover them yourself. Thinking of your life is a long, difficult journey. At some point you start running short of what you need. As you struggle on, you suddenly fall into a hole and hurt yourself. But it turns out that it's not all negative. If only you look, you'll find that right in that hole is something you've desperately needed to complete your journey successfully. And you wouldn't have found it if you hadn't fallen in that hole. As time goes on, you may even be able to say that this discovery was worth the fall.

Dr. Bryant, "There is no pain of being hurt by someone close to you. People whom you never expected to turn on you have not done so. Like a quarterback on the football field, you've been hit from the blind side, the side opposite your throwing hand an attack so unexpected you never saw it coming. Attacks like that drain you. They leave you without the energy to cry and so mad you are numb, especially when you've been wounded by your own friends, your family, someone who you had confidence and with whom you let down your guard and we ought to understand that all of us are under attack, and it is not until we fight for one another that we as the body of Christ will be able to win." [151]

---

[151] Jamal Bryant *World War Me*. (Baltimore. Empowerment. 2009), 70.

God does not put the light into us until we are broken. This means some of the things that wounded you were school for you. God was teaching and training you in the middle of your pain so you could learn what you could live with and what you could do without. I am going to put the light in you so that when your enemies are far off, they will not be able to see you but they will see the light in you," God says, There are people looking at you and wondering how you've been able to keep it together even when life has been falling apart,

These are actual cases that came through CHM's center. After working with their present law firms and making suggestions, out of 100 percent of the clients that followed this process, we had 90% success rate and the results predicted at the beginning stages were the outcome of each situations. There were numerous clients that requested that their information not be included in the interviews for this dissertation. 90% of those clients also had the same type of success in getting the planned results.

We do understand that this is a fairly new and cutting edge project so there are not a lot of statistics.

CASE STUDIES
CLIENT: Susan Holmes

CASE: Foreclosure

SITUATION: Client was facing foreclosure on her home.

CHALLENGES: Ms. Holmes had suffered a financial loss and fell behind on her mortgage payments. Although Ms. Holmes previously consulted with an attorney, the attorney failed to file the necessary motions for violation of the Bankruptcy Code 11 USC 362, Automatic Stay. Because of this action, the lender changed the locks on the doors of her home for a period of six months.

ACTIONS: Ms. Holmes was referred to CHMCLACCC to assist her with this matter. The action taken was there was a motion filed for sanctions against the bank for the automatic stay. However, the bank chose not to litigate, but to settle.

Ms. Holmes was very emotional and upset when she came to us. Our first step was for her to fill out the necessary intake paperwork to decipher what type of counseling she was seeking, which in this case, Ms. Holmes was looking for assistance in her bankruptcy/foreclosure.

The next step, she was given the APS test to determine her temperament. This is done to give the counselor a better understanding of the client's inborn traits.

Step three, Ms. Holmes was asked to share what she was going through and her feelings. This session also is used to find out if the client has a relationship with God. If not, He is introduced.

The client's needs and a course of action is discussed in step four to determine which needs are being met and which needs are not, so that they can be addressed.

Step five, the client's needs have been identified and an approach determined on how to meet those needs.

Step six, client is given a plan of instructions to follow to overcome this painful situation. This plan, in the case of Ms. Holmes, as well as others in this same situation, was to meet with bankruptcy attorney on staff and a real estate professional to be educated on the process of her situation and what actions could be taken.

RESULTS: Choosing Hope Ministries' attorney worked with Ms. Holmes' attorney to instruct her on the course of actions that could be taken. Those actions consisted of sanctions and fines against the lender, however; the lender chose to settle the morning of her court appearance. The results were there was $100,000 in arrears put on the back end of her loan, with no interest, for the term of five years. She was also awarded $20,000 and her mortgage was brought up to current standing. As of November 2011, Ms. Holmes' bankruptcy was discharged and she is still in possession of her home.

SUSAN HOLMES

I am a retired, disabled, navy veteran, who has served this country meticulously and meritoriously for 21 years, and a single mother. Throughout my military career, I saved my money so that one day I would be able to retire and come back to the United States of America where I planned to buy my first home. After signing the contract to purchase my new home (2006), my Mother became ill and I had to assume some of the medical financial responsibilities for her care. This caused the beginning of a financial hardship for me. I reached out to an established law firm for advice, hoping to find out what available options, if any I may have. In 2008 I had to file bankruptcy. In working with the law firm, the situation became very stressful, time consuming and costly. With the very limited knowledge that I the client have, and the expectation that the law firm would have the best interest of their paying client at heart, I continued to listen to and follow the advice of the law firm. Their advice being; I can only file a chapter 13, due to my amount of income. While filing the chapter 13, I consistently provided information to the law firm; with which they continually disregarded. I was becoming more and more frustrated and confused. During this time, I was also faced with the foreclosure of my home, for which I had to enlist the services of a second law firm. I again, the client became the victim, having had my rights taken away, a right that I earned and a right that all human beings have. The right to having a law firm represent you respectfully, and to the best of their ability, while honoring their fiduciary to the client. Having lost all faith and trust in the legal system and society, and with no progress being made, I reached out to a third law firm with the assistance of Choosing Hope Ministries Christian Legal Aid Counseling Center (CHMCLACC), with the hopes that this time, I would be able to get a resolution that would prove favorable for me. The founder of CHMCLACC, Dr. Ronnie Moore, immediately sprang into action. CHMCLACC is a very empathic organization that truly meets the needs of God's people. Throughout the entire, chaotic, disastrous situation with the first and second law firms, CHMCLACC a consultant, and trusted confidant, was very supportive with providing positive information in regards to options that were available to me throughout the course of the filing of the bankruptcy; such as filing chapter 7 verses a chapter 13. When this option was presented to the law firm, again, I was told, due to my income, this option was not available. CHMCLACC stood by me and gave me the strength to stay the course with the law firm, and make them do their job.

With the information provided to me, information that I believe the law firms withheld from me, the client, I began to feel that there was hope after all. On an appearance before the judge, the judge raised the question; 'Why hasn't this client filed a chapter 7 verses a chapter 13?". This was in alignment with the competent information that CHMCLACC provided me through the legal aid counseling center. A question still remains in my mind, why didn't the law firms that I paid divulge this information? CHMCLACC was able to resolve my bankruptcy resulting in a long awaited discharge. CHMCLACC restored my dignity, while strengthening my faith. I am now facing job loss, fore- which I again am seeking assistance from CHMCLACC. For without CHMCLACC I would not know what would have happened to my son and me or where we might be." I Thank God for CHMCLACC".

CHMCLACC CASE STUDY

CLIENT: Jeffrey DeBow

CASE: Suing a Law School

SITUATION: Law school refused to degree.

CHALLENGES: Mr. DeBow came to CHMCLACC because after completing the necessary three and a half years of study as well as his dissertation, which he received an A grade, GPA of 3.5, graduating in the top 3% of the class, he was denied his degree due to an agreement which was not acceptable, that caused a discharge of balance due to the lack of the law school failing to provide a reaffirmation agreement to the court for approval.

ACTIONS: Mr. DeBow came to CHMCLACC under much duress. His initial intake forms were completed on his first visit.

The next step, he was given the APS test to determine his temperament. This is done to give the counselor a better understanding of the client's inborn traits.

Step three, Mr. DeBow was asked to share what he was going through and his feelings. This session also is used to find out if the client has a relationship with God. If not, He is introduced.

The client's needs and a course of action is discussed in step four to determine which needs are being met and which needs are not, so that they can be addressed.

Step five, the client's needs have been identified and an approach determined on how to meet those needs.

Step six, client is given a plan of instructions to follow to overcome this painful situation. This plan, in the case of Mr. DeBow, he was given the opportunity to meet with our staff attorney to discuss the appropriate measure to take in order to receive his degree.

RESULTS: A motion was filed for sanctions and violation of the automatic stay. The judge ordered the law school to pay a sum of $10,000 or award Mr. DeBow his degree within thirty days. Mr. DeBow received his degree in thirteen days.

CHMCLACC CASE STUDY

CLIENT: Janene Brownlee

CASE: Workers Compensation

SITUATION: After three surgeries on her cervical spine, the insurance agency representing Ms. Brownlee's employer offered her a mere $20,000 as her reward.

CHALLENGES: Ms. Brownlee suffered a great deal of pain, loss of daily activities as well as a great financial loss.

ACTIONS: Ms. Brownlee came to CHMCLACC seeking assistance with this matter.

Ms. Brownlee was very emotional and upset when she came to us. Our first step was for her to fill out the necessary intake paperwork to decipher what type of counseling she was seeking, which in this case, Ms. Brownlee was looking for assistance in her workers compensation case.

The next step, she was given the APS test to determine her temperament. This is done to give the counselor a better understanding of the client's inborn traits.

Step three, Ms. Brownlee was asked to share what she was going through and her feelings. This session also is used to find out if the client has a relationship with God. If not, He is introduced.

The client's needs and a course of action is discussed in step four to determine which needs are being met and which needs are not, so that they can be addressed.

Step five, the client's needs have been identified and an approach determined on how to meet those needs.

Step six, client is given a plan of instructions to follow to overcome this painful situation. This plan, in the case of Ms. Brownlee met with the attorney on staff to go over her case. CHMCLACC met with an attorney specializing in Workers Compensation cases and together, they came up with a plan to seek additional compensation for the client. After sending a letter to the commissioner, the commissioner denied the initial offer from the insurance company because their offer was not acceptable.

RESULTS: After CHMCLACC's attorney's meeting with the Workers Compensation lawyer, a demand letter was sent to the insurance company requesting additional financial compensation for the client. The insurance company finally agreed and Ms. Brownlee was paid an additional $60,000 for her pain and suffering.

CHMCLACC CASE STUDY

CLIENT: Alice Wagner

CASE: Bench Warrant

SITUATION: Ms. Wagner was facing a court appearance for a bench warrant regarding a bad check charge

CHALLENGES: Ms. Wagner received word that she would be arrested for an outstanding warrant for a fraudulent check. This happened the day before Thanksgiving and Ms. Wagner was afraid that she would be locked up over the holiday and be away from her children.

ACTIONS: Ms. Wagner came to CHMCLACC under much duress. Her initial intake forms were completed on her first visit.

The next step, she was given the APS test to determine her temperament. This is done to give the counselor a better understanding of the client's inborn traits.

Step three, Ms. Wagner was asked to share what she was going through and her feelings. This session also is used to find out if the client has a relationship with God. If not, He is introduced.

The client's needs and a course of action is discussed in step four to determine which needs are being met and which needs are not, so that they can be addressed.

Step five, the client's needs have been identified and an approach determined on how to meet those needs.

Step six, client is given a plan of instructions to follow to overcome this painful situation. This plan, in the case of Ms. Wagner, she first met with our counselors to discuss her emotional state during this period as well as sit in on group therapy and share what she was experiencing with others going through similar situations. The spiritual counseling sessions are attended by all clients seeking assistance at CHMCLACC.

RESULTS: After the police officer was contacted by CHMCLACCC, he held up on serving the warrant with the understanding that Dr. Moore will bring Ms. Wagner to court the following Monday morning instead of her being confined over the weekend. The case was presented to the judge on Monday morning and the judge recommended community service, repayment of fine and court costs/restitution and after six months, the charges were wiped from her record.

CHMCLACC CASE STUDY

CLIENT: Duke Bens

CASE: Eviction

SITUATION: Mr. Duke Bens was locked out of his rental property, (shared entry), landlord locked deadbolt on door, (agreement not to lock no key). This occurred while returning home from school.

CHALLENGES: The problem is a court order is needed to evict.

ACTIONS: Mr. Bens came to CHMCLACC under much stress. His initial intake forms were completed on his first visit and a decision was made as to what type of assistance would be needed. He was concerned if he went about being charged with trespassing if he attempted to retrieve his belongings. Defending this lawsuit would cost far more than evicting the tenant using legal court procedures.

The next step, he was given the APS test to determine his temperament. This is done to give the counselor a better understanding of the client's inborn traits.

Step three, Mr. Duke Bens was asked to share what he was going through and his feelings. This session also is used to find out if the client has a relationship with God. If not, He is introduced.

The client's needs and a course of action is discussed in step four to determine which needs are being met and which needs are not, so that they can be addressed.

Step five, the client's needs have been identified and an approach determined on how to meet those needs. Mr. Bens was instructed to produce a copy of his signed leasing agreement. At this point, the landlord was contacted by CHMCLACC and told that what he was doing was illegal and he would be held accountable for any damage to Mr. Bens' property as well as his pain and suffering.

Step six, client is given a plan of instructions to follow to overcome this painful situation. This plan, in the case of Mr. Bens, was for him to contact his local police department and request that they accompany him when he returned to the apartment.

RESULTS: Within an hour after being contacted by CHMCLACC, Mr. Bens was able to return to his home. Mr. Bens saved a $2,000.00 retainer from the start.

CHMCLACC CASE STUDY

CLIENT : Bob Sonjohn

CASE: Alleged assault

SITUATION: Mr. Sonjohn was facing a criminal charge for an alleged assault

CHALLENGES: Mr. Sonjohn was attending a baseball game when a fight broke out between a relative and another bystander. Mr. Sonjohn intervened, trying to break up the fight when he accidently knocked over another bystander.

ACTIONS: Mr. Sonjohn came to CHMCLACC seeking assistance on how he should handle this situation. He was very much concerned because this would be his first contact with the police and he did not want a criminal record. His initial intake forms were completed on his first visit and it was determined that he would need to speak to the attorney on staff.

The next step, he was given the APS test to determine his temperament. This is done to give the counselor a better understanding of the client's inborn traits. The results, simply put, will show how a person will react or act in different situations they may face.

Step three, Mr. Sonjohn was asked to share what he was going through and his feelings. This session also is used to find out if the client has a relationship with God. If not, He is introduced.

The client's needs and a course of action is discussed in step four to determine which needs are being met and which needs are not, so that they can be addressed.

Step five, the client's needs have been identified and an approach determined on how to meet those needs.

Step six, client is given a plan of instructions to follow to overcome this painful situation. This plan, in the case of Mr. Sonjohn, was to consult with the attorney to discuss what measures he could take in order to have this charged dismissed. He was asked to produce the name/s of any one who may have witnessed this altercation. The attorney contacted several witnesses to get their side of the story and they each corroborated what Mr. Sonjohn had said

RESULTS: Mr. Sonjohn was given a court date to answer these charges. After reviewing the witness statements, the charges against Mr. Sonjohn were dropped.

CHMCLACC CASE STUDY

CLIENT: Romo Drake

CASE: Substance Abuse Counseling

SITUATION: Mr. Drake wanted to overcome his addiction and become a better father and husband.

CHALLENGES: Mr. Drake was referred by the courts to get counseling to treat his addiction, which at this point, was becoming a problem on his job and interfering in his family relationships.

ACTIONS: Mr. Drake came to CHMCLACC seeking help with his addiction. His initial intake forms were completed on his first visit.

The next step, he was given the APS test to determine his temperament. This is done to give the counselor a better understanding of the client's inborn traits.

Step three, Mr. Drake was asked to share what he was going through and his feelings. This session also is used to find out if the client has a relationship with God. If not, He is introduced.

The client's needs and a course of action is discussed in step four to determine which needs are being met and which needs are not, so that they can be addressed.

Step five, the client's needs have been identified and an approach determined on how to meet those needs.

Step six, client is given a plan of instructions to follow to overcome this painful situation. This plan, in the case of Mr. Drake, he was scheduled to attend daily meetings with our drug addiction counselor as well as group therapy sessions three times a week. One main issue Mr. Drake was facing was how to change his living environment. He resided with two other roommates and they each were involved in the drug culture.

CHMCLACC contacted a few of their members who owned rental properties and secured an apartment for Mr. Drake. This was a major step because Mr. Drake felt if he stayed in his current environment, he would not be able to beat his addiction.

RESULTS: Mr. Drake moved into the new apartment and continues to attend meetings. He does not go on a daily basis, but makes sure he sees his counselor a minimum of three times a week. Mr. Drake also enrolled in college to become an addictions counselor. As of August 2009, Mr. Drake has remained sober, is still on his job and is doing very well. He also volunteers a few hours a week at a homeless shelter where he speaks to the young people about the dangers of drug use.

CHMCLACC CASE STUDY

CLIENT: Dow Denbran

CASE: Anger Management

SITUATION: Mr. Denbran seemed to be very angry at the least little situation. He felt that he was becoming out of control.

CHALLENGES: Mr. Denbran had been in an altercation on his job and was suspended without pay for three weeks and it was determined that in order for him to keep his job, he would have to attend counseling for his anger.

ACTIONS: When Mr. Denbran came to CHMCLACC, it was very apparent that he needed help containing his anger. His initial intake forms were completed on his first visit. It was decided that he would be enrolled in the Anger Management classes, which were held three nights a week

The next step, he was given the APS test to determine his temperament. This is done to give the counselor a better understanding of the client's inborn traits.

Step three, Mr. Denbran was asked to share what he was going through and his feelings. This session also is used to find out if the client has a relationship with God. If not, He is introduced.

The client's needs and a course of action is discussed in step four to determine which needs are being met and which needs are not, so that they can be addressed.

Step five, the client's needs have been identified and an approach determined on how to meet those needs.

Step six, client is given a plan of instructions to follow to overcome this painful situation. This plan, in the case of Mr. Debran, the first thing that had to happen was to get to the reason why he was so angry. Although he was a very decent man, the littlest thing would cause him to go off. During one of the sessions, Mr. Denbran shared that he had grown up in foster care and because of the treatment he received in some of those homes, he became an angry young man.

RESULTS: After opening up about his childhood, it was determined that Mr. Denbran had never forgiven his mother for allowing him to live in these conditions. Mr. Debran was reminded that his mother was also going through an addiction problem and felt that giving him up would allow him to have a better life than she could give him. As a child, the only thing he thought was she just didn't want him anymore. And this is where is anger began.

Mr. Debran, after many counseling sessions, finally came to the realization that in order for him to move past this painful situation, he first had to forgive his mother for her actions. This does not say he would forget, but he had to forgive her and let it go. He eventually was ready to sit down and speak to her to get her side of the story. This was very emotional for the two of them. However, it gave him a better understanding of what his mother was going through, and together, they now attend counseling sessions to work on their relationship. His anger is now under control because he was able to let that past hurt go and looked forward to establishing a mother-son relationship with his mom.

CHMCLACC CASE STUDY

CLIENT: LaMal Mitch

SITUATION: Car Accident/DUI

CHALLENGES: Mr. Mitch was facing charges for a car accident and driving under the influence. Mr. Mitch states that he was not under the influence of any illegal drugs at the time of the accident, but instead, had taken a prescribed cough syrup approximately 2 hours before the accident.

ACTIONS: Mr. Mitch was referred to CHMCLACC by a friend's parents who were on the board. His initial intake forms were completed on his first visit and it the discussion was made as to what type of services he would need. Mr. Mitch was referred to sit down with the staff attorney to discuss his case.

The next step, he was given the APS test to determine his temperament. This is done to give the counselor a better understanding of the client's inborn traits.

Step three, Mr. Mitch was asked to share what he was going through and his feelings. This session also is used to find out if the client has a relationship with God. If not, He is introduced.

The client's needs and a course of action is discussed in step four to determine which needs are being met and which needs are not, so that they can be addressed.

Step five, the client's needs have been identified and an approach determined on how to meet those needs.

Step six, client is given a plan of instructions to follow to overcome this painful situation. This plan, in the case of Mr. Mitch, met with the attorney and was instructed to first, present his medical record to prove that he had been prescribed this medication by a licensed doctor.

RESULTS: CHMCLACC was able to get a statement from the doctor. This statement proved that the medication taken by Mr. Mitch, did not have any narcotics in the ingredients, but a possible side effect could make an individual dizzy. This is what happened with Mr. Mitch. The prosecutor decided to drop the DUI charge and Mr. Mitch was ordered to pay for the damage to the parked car that he hit. Mr. Mitch was very satisfied with the outcome of his case.

CHMCLACC CASE STUDY

CLIENT: Vet Dioh

SITUATION: Denial of Social Security Benefits

CHALLENGES: Mr. Dioh sustained a permanent injury to his back in an accident and unable to work. He was denied benefits.

ACTIONS: Mr. Dioh came to CHMCLACC to get assistance in filing to receive SSI Disability benefits and was very upset. His initial intake forms were completed on his first visit.

The next step, he was given the APS test to determine his temperament. This is done to give the counselor a better understanding of the client's inborn traits.

Step three, Mr. Dioh was asked to share what he was going through and his feelings. This session also is used to find out if the client has a relationship with God. If not, He is introduced.

The client's needs and a course of action is discussed in step four to determine which needs are being met and which needs are not, so that they can be addressed.

Step five, the client's needs have been identified and an approach determined on how to meet those needs.

Step six, client is given a plan of instructions to follow to overcome this painful situation. This plan, in the case of Mr. Dioh, he met with one of our volunteer attorneys and was told to bring in copies of all of his medical records. These would be needed to prove to the courts that he truly had a permanent injury that kept him from employment.

RESULTS: Mr. Dioh was given a hearing date, which the attorney attended with him. After submitting the corroborating evidence, Mr. Dioh was given an appointment to see one of the SSI's doctors to be examined. It was found that his injury qualified him to receive these benefits. Normally, this could take a year or more, but with the assistance of CHM, his benefits were awarded to him within nine months.

CHMCLACC CASE STUDY

CLIENT: Morea DeBello

SITUATION: Personal Injury

CHALLENGES: Ms. DeBello was a passenger in a car that was involved in an accident where she received an injury to her back.

ACTIONS: Ms. DeBello came to CHMCLACC because she had been unsuccessful in getting the insurance to pay her PIP claim. The initial intake forms were completed on her first visit.

The next step, she was given the APS test to determine her temperament. This is done to give the counselor a better understanding of the client's inborn traits.

Step three, Ms. DeBello was asked to share what he was going through and her feelings. This session also is used to find out if the client has a relationship with God. If not, He is introduced.

The client's needs and a course of action is discussed in step four to determine which needs are being met and which needs are not, so that they can be addressed.

Step five, the client's needs have been identified and an approach determined on how to meet those needs.

Step six, client is given a plan of instructions to follow to overcome this painful situation. This plan, in the case of Ms. DeBello, she was given the opportunity to meet with our staff attorney to discuss the appropriate measure to take in order to receive the compensation for her injuries. She was instructed to bring in all of her medical records, any receipts of payment to doctors/prescriptions, a copy of the accident report and the declaration page of the vehicle owner's insurance coverage.

RESULTS: The attorney sent a demand letter to the insurance company that also included copies of her records, receipts and any pertinent information to this case. The letter also stated that the insurance company was in violation of the laws of the state which says they have 30 days to pay such a claim and if they did not release these funds to her within the next 7 business days, a motion for sanction will be filed. Ms. DeBello received her money by day six.

CHMCLACC CASE STUDY

CLIENT: Dobie Howell

CASE: Child Support

SITUATION: Mr. Howell was ordered to pay child support for a child that was not his.

CHALLENGES: Mr. Howell had been in a relationship with the child's mother for approximately 3 years. At the time, they were engaged so he believed he was the child's father. However, after breaking up, he was informed that he may not be the biological father and requested a DNA, which proved he was not the dad.

ACTIONS: On his first visit, he completed the necessary intake forms and an agreement made for him to speak to someone from the legal staff.

The next step, he was given the APS test to determine his temperament. This is done to give the counselor a better understanding of the client's inborn traits.

Step three, Mr. Howell was asked to share what he was going through and his feelings. This session also is used to find out if the client has a relationship with God. If not, He is introduced.

The client's needs and a course of action is discussed in step four to determine which needs are being met and which needs are not, so that they can be addressed.

Step five, the client's needs have been identified and an approach determined on how to meet those needs.

Step six, client is given a plan of instructions to follow to overcome this painful situation. This plan, in the case of Mr. Howell, he was given the opportunity to meet with our staff attorney to discuss the appropriate measure to take in order to correct this. Because Mr. Howell ability to afford a DNA test, this was ordered and it was proven that he was not the biological child. However, because he had been in the father role, we asked if he had any evidence that the mother knew there was a possibility that he was not the father. He was able to produce a copy of a text message that she sent him in angst, stating "that's why you're not his real father….."

RESULTS: Mr. Howell was instructed to go to the court and request a hearing. After producing the results of the DNA test, as well as submitting a copy of the text message he received, the order was lifted by the judge and Mr. Howell could cease in sending in his monthly payments.

CHMCLACC CASE STUDY

CLIENT: Miles Nordet

CASE: Home Refinance

SITUATION: Mr. Nordet was getting behind on his mortgage and was seeking assistance in how to refinance his home.

CHALLENGES: Mr. Nordet was not aware of how to go about refinancing his mortgage or receiving some of the equity that was in his home. One lender he contacted wanted to charge him $8,000 in order for him to receive $15,000.

ACTIONS: Mr. Nordet came to CHMCLACC for assistance in his home refinancing. His initial intake forms were completed on his first visit. It was determined that he would be meeting with the real estate professional on staff.

The next step, he was given the APS test to determine his temperament. This is done to give the counselor a better understanding of the client's inborn traits.

Step three, Mr. Nordet was asked to share what he was going through and his feelings. This session also is used to find out if the client has a relationship with God. If not, He is introduced.

The client's needs and a course of action is discussed in step four to determine which needs are being met and which needs are not, so that they can be addressed.

Step five, the client's needs have been identified and an approach determined on how to meet those needs.

Step six, client is given a plan of instructions to follow to overcome this painful situation. This plan, in the case of Mr. Nordet, he was given the opportunity to meet with our staff professional to discuss the appropriate measure to take. Mr. Nordet was given a crash course in how the refinancing programs worked and which ones to stay away from.

RESULTS: After the learning the process and researching different banks and financial institutions, Mr. Nordet was able to choose an organization that had the best deals as well as the best interest rates. Mr. Nordet was able to refinance his home and for the same $8,000, would be able to get $50,000 in equity out of his home.

CHMCLACC CASE STUDY

CLIENT: Mann Blessed

CASE: Separation/Divorce

SITUATION: Mr. Blessed came to the center seeking assistance in how to go about filing the necessary papers to obtain a separation.

CHALLENGES: The greatest challenge Mr. Blessed was facing was he still loved his wife and really wanted his marriage to work out.

ACTIONS: Mr. Blessed came to CHMCLACC under much duress. His initial intake forms were completed on his first visit and he was scheduled to meet with one of our counselors on staff.

The next step, he was given the APS test to determine his temperament. This is done to give the counselor a better understanding of the client's inborn traits.

Step three, Mr. Blessed was asked to share what he was going through and his feelings. This session also is used to find out if the client has a relationship with God. If not, He is introduced.

The client's needs and a course of action is discussed in step four to determine which needs are being met and which needs are not, so that they can be addressed.

Step five, the client's needs have been identified and an approach determined on how to meet those needs.

Step six, client is given a plan of instructions to follow to overcome this painful situation. This plan, in the case of Mr. Blessed, he began weekly one-one-one counseling sessions with his counselor. During these sessions, he revealed that he was also dealing with the fact that he may be losing his job due to a downsizing, something he had not revealed to his wife. He revealed that he was taking out his frustrations on his wife, which he realized was wrong. He also realized that he was being unfair in his treatment of her.

He was instructed to bring his wife to the next counseling session. In this session, she also revealed that she'd noticed his change in attitude but had no clue what was going on because he chose not to share this information with her. She was happy to know that what they were going through, they could get past it if he was willing to continue the counseling sessions. At this point, they decided to come into marriage counseling together as well as join the couple's ministry at their local church.

RESULTS: Mr. and Mrs. Blessed continued their counseling sessions, together and one-on-one. They both came to the agreement that it was the best thing they could have done. They were able to communicate their feelings to each other without blaming the other party. They were also willing to accept their faults and work on them together. They also learned quite a bit about the other during these sessions. Today, Mr. and Mrs. Blessed are still together and very active in their church's couple's ministry.

CHMCLACC CASE STUDY

CLIENT: Susan Cunningham

CASE: Juvenile Delinquent

SITUATION: A single mother, Ms. Cunningham's fourteen year old son was facing charges for trespassing and was not attending school regularly.

CHALLENGES: Ms. Cunningham came to the center to discuss getting counseling and/or mentorship for her son, who was on the verge of getting expelled from school for truancy and had a trespassing charge against him.

ACTIONS: The first step was to get the initial intake forms completed. Since he is a juvenile, Ms. Cunningham was allowed to attend his sessions.

The next step, Ms. Cunningham's son was given the APS test to determine his temperament. This is done to give the counselor a better understanding of the client's inborn traits.

Step three, was asked to share what he was going through and his feelings. This session also is used to find out if the client has a relationship with God. If not, He is introduced.

The client's needs and a course of action is discussed in step four to determine which needs are being met and which needs are not, so that they can be addressed.

Step five, the client's needs have been identified and an approach determined on how to meet those needs.

Step six, client is given a plan of instructions to follow to overcome this painful situation. The plan for this young man consisted of him to continue counseling sessions, write a letter of apology to his mother regarding his actions, and spending time with one of the mentors at CHMCLACCC.

RESULTS: At the beginning of his sessions, "David" tried his best to continue his "bad boy" behavior thinking this made him a "man." However, after meeting with his mentor, he was educated on the true facts of having that type of lifestyle. David's mentor had a friend, who had served almost 12 years in prison, come in and speak to David about his own experiences. David was told of how bad prison really is. How he had to fight just to stay alive, how terrible the food was and even worse, how unsanitary the bathrooms/showers were. The stories told to David that day opened his eyes about the real world.

A meeting was set up with the principle of David's school to see what could be done to get him caught up with his classmates. David would only be allowed to return to school once he completed a semester at an alternative school. After completion of his semester, David returned to his school with a new attitude about life and how he wanted to live it. David's grades improved tremendously, his relationship with his mother was on the mend and he no longer hangs out with those friends.

As far as the trespassing charge, the staff attorney met with the prosecutor and the prosecutor agreed not to take this to court as long as David continued and completed his counseling sessions.

CHMCLACC CASE STUDY

CLIENT: Rosa Garcia
CASE: Eviction

SITUATION: Client was facing an eviction from her rental property.

CHALLENGES: Ms. Garcia received an illegal eviction notice from her landlord. Ms. Garcia was 3 months into a one-year lease when her landlord decided he wanted to rent his home to a family member. He came up with some untruths about his tenant, hoping to scare her into moving out. Ms. Garcia felt that she was a victim of discrimination.

ACTIONS: Ms. Garcia came in and completed her intake paperwork and to see what type of counseling she would need.

.The next step, she was given the APS test to determine her temperament. This is done to give the counselor a better understanding of the client's inborn traits.

Step three, Ms. Garcia was asked to share what she was going through and her feelings. This session also is used to find out if the client has a relationship with God. If not, He is introduced.

The client's needs and a course of action is discussed in step four to determine which needs are being met and which needs are not, so that they can be addressed.

Step five, the client's needs have been identified and an approach determined on how to meet those needs.

Step six, client is given a plan of instructions to follow to overcome this painful situation. Ms. Garcia met with the staff attorney and was told to bring in all necessary paperwork, complaints, etc. to disprove the allegations levied against her by her landlord.

RESULTS: After reviewing the documents, the staff attorney sent a letter to Ms. Garcia's landlord instructing him that what he was doing was illegal and he could face charges. He did not have the right to just evict someone under false pretenses and if he wanted to continue this action, he would have to file the necessary paperwork with the courts.

The landlord was also informed that this situation truly was a case of discrimination and if he chose to continue, he would face charges for that as well. At this point, he withdrew his eviction and Ms. Garcia remained on the premises for the remainder of her lease

CHMCLACC CASE STUDY

CLIENT: Wainwright Tinsdale

CASE: Grief Counseling

SITUATION: Mr. Tinsdale was depressed after the death of his wife.

CHALLENGES: Mr. Tinsdale's wife was killed in an automobile accident which left him with a permanent injury. He felt quite guilty because his wife did not survive and he did, even though the accident was not his fault.

ACTIONS: Mr. Tindale's initial intake forms were completed on his first visit and a decision was made as to what type of counseling he would be receiving.

The next step, he was given the APS test to determine his temperament. This is done to give the counselor a better understanding of the client's inborn traits.

Step three, Mr. Tinsdale was asked to share what he was going through and his feelings. This session also is used to find out if the client has a relationship with God. If not, He is introduced.

The client's needs and a course of action is discussed in step four to determine which needs are being met and which needs are not, so that they can be addressed.

Step five, the client's needs have been identified and an approach determined on how to meet those needs.

Step six, client is given a plan of instructions to follow to overcome this painful situation. This plan, in the case of Mr. Tinsdale, he first met with our counselors to discuss his emotional state during this period as well as sit in on group therapy and share what he was experiencing with others going through similar situations. The spiritual counseling sessions are attended by all clients seeking assistance at CHMCLACC.

RESULTS: During the group counseling sessions is where Mr. Tinsdale was able to hear stories that resembled his. He came to the realization that he was not alone and most people in his situation felt the same kind of guilt and depression. It took him a few weeks before he was able to get up and speak on his personal situation, but after getting through that tearful moment, he began to feel better through prayer and fellowshipping with those who shared not only his belief in Christ, but his own personal experience.

Mr. Tinsdale decided that the more he talked about his experience, the better he felt, so at this time, Mr. Tinsdale is a volunteer speaker at some of our group meetings. He has become quite an asset to those facing similar situations.

CHMCLACC CASE STUDY

CLIENT: Kristal Anderson

CASE: Child Support

SITUATION: Ms. Anderson, a single mother of two, was unsuccessful in trying to file paperwork to receive child support.

CHALLENGES: Ms. Anderson attempted to file the necessary form to seek child support from her ex-boyfriend, who is the father of her two children. He is now denying and wants a paternity test to prove that he is the father.

ACTIONS: Ms. Anderson came to CHMCLACC seeking assistance with this matter. She knew that she could not afford to have the test done, and the ex-boyfriend was counting on this. Ms. Anderson was quite angry and upset when she came to us. Our first step was for her to fill out the necessary intake paperwork to decipher what type of counseling she was seeking, which in this case, Ms. Anderson was looking for assistance in filing the necessary forms to receive child support.

The next step, she was given the APS test to determine her temperament. This is done to give the counselor a better understanding of the client's inborn traits.

Step three, Ms. Anderson was asked to share what she was going through and her feelings. This session also is used to find out if the client has a relationship with God. If not, He is introduced.

The client's needs and a course of action is discussed in step four to determine which needs are being met and which needs are not, so that they can be addressed.

Step five, the client's needs have been identified and an approach determined on how to meet those needs.

Step six, client is given a plan of instructions to follow to overcome this painful situation. This plan, in the case of Ms. Anderson, she met with the attorney on staff to see what course of action she could take. The first step was to file the necessary forms, with the attorney's assistance, with the Department of Social Services.

RESULTS: After filing the forms, Ms. Anderson was scheduled for a court hearing for her to address the court. After relaying that she and the ex-boyfriend had been together for over five years and producing copies of the birth certificates, which had his signature, the judge ordered him to take a blood test, at his expense, or face a contempt charge. The results showed that he was indeed the father of both children and ordered to pay Ms. Anderson monthly child support as well as paying the arrears for the previous years.

CHMCLACC CASE STUDY

CLIENT: Teresa Belt

SITUATION: Ms. Belt purchased a brand new car from the dealership. However, the car kept having break down after break down and was taken in to service 6 times within the first 8 months.

CHALLENGES: Ms. Belt tried unsuccessfully to solve this problem with the dealership but kept getting the run around.

ACTIONS: Ms. Belt sought assistance from CHMCLACC after being referred by a coworker. The first step was for her to fill out the necessary intake paperwork to decipher what type of counseling she was seeking, which in this case, Ms. Belt was looking for assistance in her car situation, which she felt was a violation of the lemon law.

The next step, she was given the APS test to determine her temperament. This is done to give the counselor a better understanding of the client's inborn traits.

Step three, Ms. Belt was asked to share what she was going through and her feelings. This session also is used to find out if the client has a relationship with God. If not, He is introduced.

The client's needs and a course of action is discussed in step four to determine which needs are being met and which needs are not, so that they can be addressed.

Step five, the client's needs have been identified and an approach determined on how to meet those needs.

Step six, client is given a plan of instructions to follow to overcome this painful situation. This plan, in the case of Ms. Belt was she met with the attorney on staff and one of our professionals who sold cars for 20 years. They determined that she was being treated unfairly and sent a letter to the general manager of the dealership requesting that Ms. Belt be put in another vehicle. They also requested that she should be awarded some sort of compensation for her hardship of having to miss days off of work to continue bringing the vehicle in for service.

RESULTS: Ms. Belt was not only given a new vehicle, the manager also revised her contract and lowered her interest rates, which gave her a lower monthly payment. So far, Ms. Belt is happy with the outcome of this situation and continues to drive her car.

CHMCLACC CASE STUDY

CLIENT: Kendra Washington

CASE: Possession of Marijuana

SITUATION: Ms.Washington was a emancipated 17 year old young lady trying to live out on her own. Her own mother had left the country and she did not have a great relationship with her father. She ended up staying with a boyfriend, who was dealing drugs. When the police raided his home, Ms. Washington was also arrested and charged.

CHALLENGES: Ms. Washington was referred to the center by an employee of the detention center. She was in desperate need of legal assistance as well as life-skills counseling services..

ACTIONS: The first step was to get the initial intake forms completed. Since she is a juvenile, a social worker also sat in on her first few sessions..

The next step, Miss Washington was given the APS test to determine his temperament. This is done to give the counselor a better understanding of the client's inborn traits.

Step three, she was asked to share what she was going through and her feelings. This session also is used to find out if the client has a relationship with God. If not, He is introduced.

The client's needs and a course of action is discussed in step four to determine which needs are being met and which needs are not, so that they can be addressed.

Step five, the client's needs have been identified and an approach determined on how to meet those needs.

Step six, client is given a plan of instructions to follow to overcome this painful situation. The plan for this young lady was to come into counseling three days a week to meet with the counselor to discuss ways she could make better decisions about her life. The counselor took into concern that she was still a child with no real direction. It was revealed that she had no place else to stay so she felt trapped to stay with this boyfriend. Even though she knew it was not a good place for her to be.

The counselor made calls to area shelters and a room was found for Miss Washington. Miss Washington was also enrolled in a GED program to get her diploma. She was then referred to the staff attorney to speak about the charges levied against her and how they would fight these charges. Although she knew what her boyfriend was doing, she had not participated in any of his illegal activities.

RESULTS: Given the age of Miss Washington and the unfortunate predicament she found herself in, the juvenile judge allowed her to continue residing at the shelter and to complete her GED program. She was also instructed to have no contact with the boyfriend. The judge was very lenient with her because she realized that Miss Washington was too young to be out on her own and had not been properly prepared to make the necessary decisions regarding what was in her best interest.

As of February 2010, Miss Washington had completed her GED program and received her diploma. She is now taking courses at the local community college to get her degree in early childhood education. She also works part time at the shelter and seems to be making better decisions regarding her life and lifestyle.

Case Study Summary

CHMCLACC's goal is to offer clients assistance and meeting them at their needs. Because of the professionals on staff and the services donated by professionals, first, second and third year law students, legal secretaries and paralegals, clients are able to get grade A assistance for services at a much discounted rate. CHM's goal is to help those less fortunate obtain the best representation as possible without having to worry about the cost.

By using these professionals and volunteers, every client that comes into the center will automatically save anywhere between $2,500.00 and $5,000.00 because they are not charged as they would be if they consulted with a legal firm where they will be required to pay a retainer fee.

Dr. Ronnie Moore, founder and president of CHMCLACC also donates two hours of his time to each client.

CONCLUSION

How To Deal With Pain
"At least I can take comfort in this: Despite the Pain, I have not denied the words of the Holy One." Job 6:10

The above scripture is one used in counseling at CHMCLACC. Our model makes a committed effort to bring the clients to God when they are experiencing painful situations. They are informed that through God's words and instructions, they can be made strong again and reach the point where they are able to overcome the distresses and painful circumstances that may surround their lives.

Alford states that there is "another kind of wisdom, which is the ability to predict the consequences of certain actions…knowing that A, when followed by B, leads to C."[152] Clients learn to take a look at things around them that they may have overlooked before. By paying close attention to those actions, will allow them to have the wisdom to see where they are going in life. Just following the plan and/or instructions they receive during sessions will be a major factor in getting beyond their current situations.

---

[152] Henry *Alford How to Live: A Search for Wisdom from Old People (While They Are Still on This Earth)* (NY: Hatchette Book Group, 2009), 4.

In order to deal with pain, one must first understand the anatomy of pain. Pain comes in many forms: physical, mental, emotional. In this thesis, emotional pain will be addressed. Dealing with one's feelings is facing, accepting and working through them. There will be times when one may feel he is not strong enough, but this can come from the fear of the unknown. Once a person realizes that everyone, Christian and non-Christians alike, experiences emotional pain, it does make it a tad bit easier to accept. Another important fact one must realize is, with proper counseling and lots of prayers, he can get to the other side. However; this will take work and he must be willing and able to put in that work.

Sometimes, people will repress these negative emotions, putting them in the back of their minds and hoping to leave them there. However, this is never successful. Eventually, they will find a way to come out whether in depression, anxiety, panic, eating disorders, etc. A lot of time, people do not want to feel what they are feeling. They may be ashamed or guilty of these feelings, or, they just do not like a certain emotion. According to an article found on pinds.com, the "natural reaction is to avoid negative feelings by suppressing them, resisting them or trying to ignore them, wanting them to just go away and trying to be positive all the time."[153]

---

[153] http://pinds.com/2007/12/20/how-to-deal-with-negative-emotions/. Accessed 11 Feb. 2010

Clients at CHMCLACC are made aware that experiencing any type of negative emotion is in fact, just a part of life. Everyone on the face of this earth will experience this in some form or fashion. There is nothing that one can do stop them. However, there are many things one can to help them to get over them and move on in their lives.

One of the very first issues counselees are taught is to not give in and continue to dwell on this temporary situation. By doing this, the only thing happening is the pain will last a whole lot longer, or in some cases, get worse. The more attention one gives the painful thoughts, the more significant they will become. Sometimes clients will react negatively to a certain situation and this action will spiral downward. However, according to John Gottman, if he "pays attention to the warning signs and dangers, he will have a better change of avoiding them."[154] Clients are taught to pay more attention to what is going on around them as well as within them. When they take notice, they will begin to see exactly what is going on and hopefully, have the strength and courage to avoid those situations. Just as one may do while driving, Gottman goes on to say that all a person must do is to "learn to yield,"[155] just as you would while driving a vehicle.

---

[154] John Gottman. *Why Marriages Succeed or Fail and How You Can Make Yours Last* (NY: Simon & Schuster, 1994). 71.

[155] _____ The *Seven Principles for Making Marriage Work* (New York: Three Rivers, 1999), 113.

According to Mark Grant, thanks to the studies of the brain activity, "doctors have been able to come up with different ways to overcome pain such as SSRI antidepressants, psychological therapies such as Eye Movement Desensitization and Reprocessing."[156] But one important thing a person must be willing to do is acknowledge whatever pain they are feeling. If they are angry, accept that they are angry. If they are hurting or depressed, accept it, because these feelings just don't happen without a reason.

There are various ways clients can work through painful situations. John Maxwell points out to "avoid burnout."[157] This can be achieved by learning to see it coming and avoid it. No matter how a person may be living their life, "we are all experienced when it comes to suffering and should acknowledge that hurt, to an extent, is a part of every life."[158] No one is immune from going through painful situations but once they've acknowledged their problem, they have a better chance of overcoming them.

---

[156] Mark Grant, "Overcoming Pain." http://www.overcomingpain.com. Accessed 8 March 2010

[157] John Maxwell. *Developing the Leader Around You.* (Nashville, TN: Thomas Nelson Inc., 1995), 157.

[158] Miriam Greenspan. *Healing through the Dark Emotions* (Boston: Shambhala, 2003). 1

Clients must realize that there is no "correct" when going through a painful situation such as grieving. If a person begins to feel depressed over the loss of a loved one, this is the time for them to share those feelings with a family member, friend, clergy, etc. If they try to hold them in, even though they may not realize this is what they are doing, it can become quite destructive to their life. He must make the choice to break out of this spell and communicate exactly what it is he is experiencing. If it is shame or fear, then they must speak about the shame and fear. Many people have a hard time dealing with grief but tears can be cleansing. There is nothing wrong with crying out. If he feels the need to cry, he should do just that. Take some time to get it out. Guarantee, he will feel a whole lot better after a good cry.

No matter what a person may be facing, if he believes that Jesus is facing it with them, he should realize and feel confident that God will work it out. God is always with everyone. When God enters into the lives of His children, it is because of His glory that one becomes secure in His grace. Chris Gardner, who at one point in his life was homeless and joblessness overcame his situation by "reinventing himself." He states that "until a person gets tired of the same results, nothing will change until the person changes."[159]

---

[159] Chris Gardner. *Start Where You Are: Life Lessons in Getting from Where You Are to Where You Want to Be* (NY: Harper Collins, 2009), 4.

Jesus has made the way of access to peace with our Father by dying on the cross for our sins. Christians are able to stand fully forgiven of their sins and are all justified through Jesus Christ, our risen Lord of life. "When we realize that God loves us with our weaknesses, vulnerability and failures, we can accept them as an inevitable part of our human life."[160] At CHMCLACC, lessons are taught to clients that God loves them even when they don't think He does. He will always be with them, even in their worst of times. They just have to put their faith in Him that all will work out in the end. As Schmookler says "we are warlike not out of power, but out of weakness."[161]

In the Gospel of Matthew, Chapter eleven, Jesus tells us that all things are given to Him by the Father. Therefore, He reveals the Father to those who come to Him. Rest from the insecurity of the present world will be given to those who seek the Father in Christ. We are given real and true knowledge of fellowship with God through Christ Jesus when we yoke together with Him. Our lives become a joint venture. This is easy work in the ministries of Jesus Christ.

---

[160] Desmond Tutu *God Has a Dream: A Vision of Hope for Our Time* (NY: Doubleday, 2004), 39.

[161] Andrew Bard Schmookler *Out of Weakness: Healing the Wounds that Drive Us to War* (NY: Bantam Books, 1994), 19.

God Can Change Anything through Prayer
"I will instruct thee and teach thee in the way which thou shalt go; I will guide thee with mine eye." Psalm 32:8 KJV

One of the goals used during counseling sessions at CHMCLACC is teaching the clients that God's will be done. No matter what, the above scripture is evidence that God is our guidance and He will instruct us according to His will. All one has to do is follow Him.

"Everything God created was designed to function by certain built-in or inherent principle."[162]

---

[162] Myles Munroe, *Kingdom Principles: Preparing for Kingdom Experience and Expansion* (PA: Destiny Image Publishers, 2006), 143.

Joel Osteen states "There is a seed in you trying to take root."[163] Take the time to nurture the seed that God has put into you. Clients are made to realize that just like a garden needs tending, so does the seed that God has planted. Take the time to water it, pull out the unnecessary weeds and prune your life according to God's plan. Mr. Osteen goes on to say "Learn to be happy with who God made you to be and quite wishing you were something different."[164] Many times, clients come into the center unhappy because they are trying to live the life that their parents wanted them to live or their spouse wants them to live. If this is the case, the client will never be happy because he is trying to live according to what someone else things they should be doing. They are unhappy in their personal lives trying to make others happy. Be happy with whom you are. If others aren't receiving of the change, it's not your problem. Be yourself.

"Be anxious for nothing, but in everything by prayer and supplication, with thanksgiving, let your requests be made known to God; and the peace of God, which surpasses all understanding, will guard your hearts and minds through Christ Jesus." (Phillippians 4:6-7 KJV). This scripture teaches us that we should be patient and wait on God. If you take your burdens to Him in prayer, your prayers will be answered according to His Will.

---

[163] Joel Osteen. *Your Best Life Now*. (New York: WarnerFaith, 2004), 10.

[164] ____. Ibid. 91

In Praying the Song of Solomon, Dr. Towns states that "when we are unsettled and things become unbearable, we will go through life unsatisfied until we find our love in Christ."[165] When we reach out to God through prayer, according to T.D. Jakes, a person "must take responsibility to renew their enthusiasm by sitting down, reviewing your list and pray to God to give you the strength and for forgiveness when you slip."[166]

Prayer changes things for God's people because "all things work together for the good of those who loves the Lord, to those who are called according to His purpose. (Romans 8:26-27 KJV). There was a client that was upset because he was about to start his own business. However, although he followed all of the rules and regulations, purchased the correct permits, etc., he kept running into problem after problem. He was told to read this scripture and was a bit confused until he realized that it reads "all things." At this time, he came to understand that even if he was met with negativity, this negativity can work together for the good. "Everything by prayer" does not mean everything in the universe, but rather "all things that pertain to life and godliness." 2Peter 1:4, 11 KJV.

Richard Wurmbrand tells the story of how Russians were imprisoned for their belief in Christ, but even through the torturing and beatings, one lesson was learned and that is "the spirit is master of the body."[167]

---

[165] Elmer Towns *Praying the Proverbs Including Ecclesiastes and the Song of Solomon* (Shippensburg, PA: Destiny Image, 2006), 237.

[166] T.D. Jakes *Making Great Decisions* (NY: Atria, 2008). 33.

[167] Richard Wurmbrand *Tortured for Christ*. (Bardesville, OK: Living

However, this does not mean that we pray only for spiritual things. Prayer will certainly change material thing when that change has a spiritual benefit and value. Prayer should not and is not for satisfying physical lusts or material things, although it doesn't mean one cannot pray for material things. Jesus taught us to pray, "Give us each day, our daily bread and forgive our trespasses." (Luke 11:3-4 KJV). The main purpose of prayer is to communicate with God.

"The effective, fervent prayer of a righteous man avails much." (James 5:16 NKJV) When a righteous man prays there are more changes than he could ever imagine or comprehend. "And the prayer of faith shall save the sick, and the Lord shall raise him up; and if he have committed sins, they shall be forgiven him. (James 5:15 KJV). The sick person is not only healed, but also saved.

In the face of difficulty, most will do their best to cope with the situation, hold it together and keep going. But sometimes, they often end up carrying emotional pain that they don't know how to heal or to release. These types of experiences will be stored emotionally in their hearts, which will limit their ability to give and receive love. According to Eugene Peterson, "prayer is the most universal of all languages because prayer is used in relation to God."[168]

Sacrifice Book Company, 1967), 42.

[168] Eugene Peterson, *Eat This Book*. (Grand Rapids, MI: William B. Erdmans Publishing, 2006). 103.

It may take a while to totally understand and gain wisdom from this scripture. However; after dealing with a few painful situations in their lives and having the strength and faith to reach up to God, the clients then realized that it was only by God's Grace and Mercy that they were able to overcome and move on with their lives.

Without pain, some would not have known what they are fortunate to know now. Many would not have reached up to God, asking Him to save them. More importantly, some would not have been aware of their own faults. However, one thing that clients and counselees have come to realize is that what they may face or suffer at the expense or actions of someone else, God can always turn a bad into a good that wrong into a right, that unfairness into fairness. The test will be a testimony of His greatness.

Steps in Moving Past Pain

"And call upon me in the day of trouble; I will deliver thee, and thou shalt glorify me." Psalm 50:15

This scripture is important to the model used at CHMCLACC. When the counselee wishes to address their pain, they are first made aware that they should pray to God for the strength needed to get to the other side of their pain. By surrendering their burdens to God, it gives them a sense of peace and the strength to take the necessary steps to be successful in bringing joy back into their lives.

One important aspect used in counseling sessions at CHMCLACC is to make clients aware that in order to move past unpleasant situations, one must be willing to accept the consequences of their actions. Sometimes, a person will find themselves in dire straits because of their personal choices and must realize that "God does not take away the consequences of their actions"[169] because according to *Dare to be a Man*, these actions can actually be beneficial. They will teach one not to continuously repeat the same mistakes over and over again.

Another important step clients at CHMCLACC must be willing to take is one of preparation. As stated in Leading from the Second Chair, by Bonem and Patterson, one must realize that the "the most important aspect of preparing in advance is mental."[170] During the sessions, clients must be prepared to make the necessary changes in their lives to get to the other side of their painful situations. By just taking one day at a time, they will begin to see their progress, which gives them more of a drive to continue on.

---

[169] David Evans. *Dare to be a Man*. (New York: Penguin, 2009), 142.

[170] Mike Bonem and Ronnie Patterson. *Leading from the Second Chair*. (San Francisco: Jossey-Bass, 2005), 91.

"When you do decide to change and set out along that path, many people around you will not like it, but by changing your presence, it will challenge others to change."[171] This problem comes up more times than not. When clients come into the center to get counseling for addictions, they have all revealed that their old friends seem to change their attitudes toward them. They are reminded that they should not allow these people to continue to pull them down. They are just angry and upset because one of their drug partners has decided to make a change. However, if they see the change, see the success that their ex partner is beginning to receive, it gives them a reason to make a change in their live as well.

A few steps that the clients are taught to do is to take time to address whatever emotion/s he is experiencing. They must remind themselves that God is with them and they are not alone. Concentrate on what they are able to do to counteract the negative feelings. While working on moving on after a traumatic or painful experience, clients learn and must be willing to make a change. "Changes will eventually become new habits and it's up to the client to decide which habit they want to keep."[172] This can be done pretty simply if clients are willing to take charge and stay away from the negative things they encounter in their lives. However, some may make excuses why they can't but "excuses are an attempt to keep from facing reality…excuses can help cover failures and weakness."[173]

---

[171] Matthew Kelly. *A Call to Joy: Living in the Presence of God.* (San Francisco: Harper Collins, 1997), 183.

[172] Paul McKenna, Hugh Willbourn *How to Mend Your Broken Heart*

One thing that has come to be realized is that many clients don't want their family or loved ones to consider them as being weak. However, just because he may be down and out at this particular time, as long as he's taking the necessary steps to get past these situations, only shows just how strong they truly are. They must believe in themselves and now allow what others may think hinder their process. Phillips goes on to say that "a good excuse can be used to change the subject and divert pressure."[174] This is done by almost every client at the beginning of their sessions.

Clients tend to come up with a myriad of excuses to take the attention away from what they are really going through. Sometimes, they are embarrassed that they must reveal what's going on in their personal lives to complete strangers. At CHMCLACC, clients are made to feel as welcome and at home as possible. This will allow them to be more relaxed and "give them the courage to accept their failures, marinate their minds, heart, soul, emotions and future in grace."[175]

(New York: Three Rivers, 2003), 40.

[173] Bob Phillips *Controlling Your Emotions Before They Control You* (Eugene, OR: Harvest House Publishers, 1995), 137.

[174] ____. Ibid, 137.

[175] Mike Foster, Jud Wilhite *Deadly Viper:Character Assassins* (MI: Zondervan, 2007), 166.

"During life's most difficult moments, even a single second of recognizing and experiencing God's love and guidance can be enough to transform our direction and completely change out attitude and outlook."[176] This quote by Jampolsky is very simple. If a person is willing to give themselves to God during their weakest moments, He has the power to transform their lives and guide them to make the necessary changes to overcome whatever negative or painful situation they may be experiencing in their life.

"People who will not re-plan their lives to include the new situation in which they find themselves, end up living life on a false basis."[177] If a client's former plans are not working out the way they intended, they need to make new plans. But if he refuses to do this, the situation will never go away. Take the time to look at new ways to make the necessary changes needed to become whole again. It may be difficult, but if a person continues to do things the same way, they cannot expect different results.

---

[176] Lee Jampolsky. *Healing Together: How to Bring Peace into Your Life and the World* (Hoboken, NJ: John Wiley Sons, 2002), 193.

[177] Elizabeth Harper Neeld. *Tough Transitions: Navigating Your Way Through Difficult Times* (New York: Warner Books, 2005), 129.

Clients are taught to share these feelings with someone they trust. Sometimes, it may be hard to express, but reaching out is a major step in releasing the pain and receiving positive feedback on ways to overcome it. Some can start out by communicating in a one-one-one sessions and gradually, be able to share in group sessions. Once clients realize that there are others who are going through the same things, it gives them more confidence that they too, can overcome. Another way to move past situations that may be hindering the client's growth is to cause a "distraction of any negative or depressing thought"[178] and not allow them to become a burden.

Do not dwell on the negative and painful situations. The more a person gives attention to those feelings, the longer those feelings will be there. Of course, they must address them, but once those feelings are addressed, they must take the energy to work to move forward. This can be done by taking up a new hobby. Replace those feelings by doing something positive such as volunteering at a senior center, reading to school children, etc. When a person decides to help others, no matter how little, will surely bring joy into a person's life.

---

[178] Samuel Deep, Lyle Sussman, *Yes You Can!* (Reading, MA: Addison-Wesley, 1997), 5.

"Discovering what grounds us, what is fulfilling to us, we can look to ways to strengthen these moments."[179] When a person is going through tough times, there are ways to make them realize that this is just a temporary. By taking a look at the blessings they already have, it will allow them to use those blessings and special moments in their lives to be an encouraging factor in getting past painful situations.

Another step the clients learn is to take a step back. Don't try to rush and clear everything all at once. These things take time. Make a list of any options that are available to them and do some research. If the pain derived from something that was done to them by someone, this is the time to forgive that person. By forgiving those who may have hurt you, it allows that burden to be lifted and you can move on, but if you never forgive, that person will always have a sort of power over you because most likely, they have moved on and haven't even thought about what they've done. On the other hand, the hurt person is still carrying around that hurt. Forgive and let it go.

---

[179] Todd Kashdan *Curious? Discover the Missing Ingredient to a Fulfilling Life* (New York: William Morrow, 2009), 61.

In Reposition Yourself, Bishop T.D. Jakes asks the question: "Do you have the courage to face the dark, silently, sinister enemy that may be lurking inside of you? Do you share have the courage to confront yourself?"[180] While taking a look at where it may be, one should take a heart to heart look at what may keep us from reaching our goals. He says that although we all will face trials, it's the "power derived from life's hardships that, like an untimed punch, catches us off guard."[181] The Bishop concluded by stating "things can turn out the way you want if you are willing to hear the truth."[182] This is another key component to the functions of CHMCLACC in helping the client to move in the direction of the other side of pain.

---

[180] T.D. Jakes. *Reposition Yourself.* (New York: Atria, 2007), 10.

[181] Ibid., 31.

[182] Ibid. 10.

While working on moving on after a traumatic or painful experience, one must learn and be willing to make a change. As pointed out in How to Mend Your Broken Heart, these "changes will eventually become new habits and it's up to the client to decide which habits they want to keep."[183] In the How to Solve the People Puzzle, one is taught that the first step is learning to "recognize the problem that may if arise if one responds poorly."[184] Instead of acting out on emotions, clients are taught to take a look at the situation as if it was not their own before they make any major decisions. This will give them the opportunity to look at the entire process of what may have gotten contributed to their painful situations and give them a better outlook on how to move past it.

---

[183] Mels Carbonell. *How to Solve the People Puzzle: Understanding Personality Patterns.* (Blue Ridge, GA: Uniquely You Resources, *2008),* 90.

[184] Ibid. 233

Lawrence Powell states that "breaking free in your mind is crucial, not for God's sake, but for your own."[185] In order to be a success in their process of overcoming pain, clients learn that they must let go of the old hurt and break free from what has been holding them back. Until this is done and no matter how much counseling he receives, until this step is done, the client will never be truly free to move forward in their lives. Mr. Powell goes on to state that as "one releases the heavy burden they've been carrying, they will begin to see how valuable they are to God."[186] This feeling can come in an instant or it may take a while. But when clients have released all of the negativity and burdens, and put their trust in God to make things right, they will definitely see how valuable they are as individuals.

---

[185] Lawrence Powell. *It's Your Call* (Tulsa, OK: Victory, 2008), 55.

[186] ____. Ibid., 56.

Bishop Jakes shows why intervention is often successful because it "produces an awareness of how your behavior hurts those around you."[187] He further states that anytime you're not focused on what matters most because "you allow yourself to be distracted and numb by some feel-good urge, it's hurting those around you."[188] Sometimes, a person doesn't realize how their emotion beings greatly affect those closest to them, even when those feelings have nothing to do with that person. This further supports CHMCLACC and the quest to make individuals from one place of hurt to a place of overcoming that hurt by taking the approach to learn from past mistakes instead of walking back through a dark cave of an empty, lonely and hurtful environment. Lastly, Bishop Jakes teaches us that "the process begins with understanding how relentless and tenacious we must be in order to prevail over the adversity we confront."[189] This statement means that a person must understand who they are and how they will respond in certain situations in order to plan on how they will approach it.

In Charlene Proctor's The Women's Book of Empowerment, which offer ways to overcome the past, she says,

"Old negative thought patterns hold you prisoner, preventing you from moving forward into a positive state of mind and heart."[190]

---

[187] T.D. Jakes. *Reposition Yourself* (New York. Atria. 2007), 23.

[188] ____. Ibid. 23.

[189] T.D. Jakes. *Reposition Yourself* (New York. Atria. 2007), 32.

[190] Charlene Proctor. *The Women's Book of Empowerment*

This is the time to say: "I'm going to change my attitude." Be positive in everything you do. Although clients may find it hard to release the painful emotions, if they make the decision to forgive those around them, take those emotions and release them from their bodies, they can truly get to the other side.

Dr. Enright state's that "forgiveness is a process, through group research, it was a discovery that to say, I forgive you," is usually not enough. Although the words are said, the angry feelings return. People need to go through a process to understand their feelings; they also need to take concrete action. He goes on to say that "sometimes we forgive one person, only to discover that, there are others whom we need to forgive."[191]

Bishop Jakes states that "you can only correct what you are willing to confront."[192] The lesson taken from this is one that could be carried to the end of time, and that is "what needs to be said should be said without any consideration of parties and the things in life that needs to be faced, should be faced."[193] Bishop Jakes also states that a number of people have made the choice to live in a state of denial. Whatever the price, "they are willing to pay instead of taking on the responsibility of doing the work that is needed to confront the issues, weakness and inconsistencies in themselves and those around them."[194]

(Birminghamd, MI: Goddess Network Press, 2005), 16.

[191] Robert Enright. *Forgiveness is a Choice. A Step-by-Step Process for Resolving Anger and Restoring Hope.* (Washington D.C.: APA Life Tools, 2001), 11.

[192] T.D. Jakes. *Reposition Yourself.* (New York. Atria. 2007), 10.

Dr. North says, "Forgiving begins with pain and that we have a right to our feelings. First, we are acknowledging that the offense was unfair and will always continue to be unfair. Secondly, we have a moral right to anger. It is fair to cling to views that, people do not have a right to hurt us. We have a right to respect. Thirdly, forgiveness requires giving up something to which we have a right-namely our anger or resentment."[195] One important aspect of forgiveness that is stressed at CHMCLACC is that clients should not only forgive whomever has caused them hurt, but that forgiving also takes away the power that the other person had over him. They begin to realize that as long as they are holding on to their pain, the other person has moved on in their lives and most likely, have completely forgotten about what they may have done to cause the client's problems.

God's Make Over
"But now thus saith the Lord that created thee, O Jacob, and he that formed thee, O Israel, Fear not; for I have redeemed thee, I have called thee by thee name, thou art mine." Isaiah 42:1 KJV

---

[193] ____. Ibid. 10.

[194] ____. Ibid. 10.

[195] J. North, *Wrongdoing and Forgiveness.* Philosophy 62:499-508 (Madison, NV: University of Wisconsin Press. Madison, 1987), 25.

Using the models of CHMCLACC, the scripture is saying that God can make the changes in a person if they are willing to submit to Him. As He called Jacob and Israel, He is telling them that He will redeem them, make them over because they belong to Him. Clients are made aware that this also includes them. If they will open their hearts and be willing to be accepting, they can be changed by the grace and mercy of God Almighty. As Mr. Butler says, "There is no magic way of immediately removing painful or problematic feelings, but there are ways of lessoning or shortening their impact."[196] This can be done by breaking down what's going on in a client's life piece by piece. Nothing truly comes easy without putting in the work. But if the client wants to move past their emotional pain, they must work hard to overcome it and move forward to having a better and happier life.

"Whatever your path, whatever your destiny, whatever obstacles you face, God will lead you to victory every time."[197] When a person is going through rough patches in their lives, if he will allow himself to trust in God's plan, everything will work out for the good. He may find himself going down an uncomfortable path, but at the end, God will bring him to victory. He goes on to say "Remember, God is on your side. He was with the widow, He was with David and He will be with you."[198] Even during the lowest moments of a person's life, and even when he may not feel God's presence, He is there. His word says that He will never forsake you and this is a promise you can depend on.

[196] Gillian Butler, Tony Hope, *Managing Your Mind. The Mental Fitness Guide;* (New York, NY: Oxford University Press, 2007), 332.

Jamal Bryant states in *World War Me* that "God does not put the light into us until we are broken. This means some of the things that wounded you were school for you. God was teaching and training you in the middle of your pain so you could learn what you could live with and what you could do without. I am going to put the light in you so that when your enemies are far off, they will not be able to see you but they will see the light in you,"[199] God says, There are people looking at you and wondering how you've been able to keep it together even when life has been falling apart.

"When people try to divorce the Word of God from their life, they've turned out all the lights…they've blinded themselves."[200] Sometimes when clients are experiencing painful moments in their lives, they tend to blame God and refuse His love and guidance. However; by doing this, they are hindering their growth and missing out on the blessings that He has for him. If only they would trust in His plan and surrender to His will, will they be able to move past painful situations and being to heal. One of the twelve steps in Alcoholic Anonymous states that "there is but one ultimate authority, a loving God, as He may express Himself in our group conscience."[201]

---

[197] Jesse Duplantis. *The Everyday Visionary: Focus Your Thoughts, Change Your Life* (NY: Simon & Schuster, 2008). 142.

[198] ____. Ibid., 142.

[199] Jamal Bryant *World War Me*. (Baltimore. Empowerment). 44.

[200] Jesse Duplantis. *The Everyday Visionary: Focus Your Thoughts, Change Your Life* (NY: Simon & Schuster, 2008), 61.

[201] Alcoholics Anonymous. *Alcoholics Anonymous: Big Book 4th Ed.*

"We need God's Big Picture perspective on our lives and our world."[202] A person may have reservations about where they're going in his life, but if he can try to take a look at the big picture that God has for him, it will make his steps a whole lot easier to take. But this only comes with being able to trust in God and His plans for our lives. We may not be able to see it, but God is working in each of His children.

In the book The Bond, the story of Maurice is proof that God can and will change a negative situation into something positive. Because of his choices, Maurice turned to a life of crime. However it took him spending time in jail that he realized he was blessed. He says that "I believe in God and where he leads me is where I'm supposed to go."[203] This is the attitude that shows if you allow it, God will make you over. There have been a few clients that came through CHMCLACC who were once incarcerated. It wasn't until then that they came to know God. Each has confessed that if they had not been locked up, they may not have taken the time to get to know God. But due to boredom, they were almost forced to read the Bible. However, they all came to the same conclusion that they all learned a lot about their own lives by reading about the lives of the people in the Bible.

(NY: AA, 2001), 563.

[202] Ben Carson with Gregg Lewis. *The Big Picture* (Grand Rapids, MI: Zondervan Publishing House, 1999), 198.

[203] Sampson Davis, George Jenkins and Rameck Hunt. *The Bond*. (New York. Penguin, 2008), 180.

God has a plan for all of His children's lives. According to scripture: "Before I formed you in the womb I knew you, before you were born I set you apart; I appointed you as a prophet to the nations...." (Jeremiah 1:5 NIV). Clients are taught to realize that their lives were planned from the very beginning. Lawrence Powell's *It's Your Call* tells us that we are being "prepared by God to do great things and that life's past struggles, albeit rough, you are still here because of God's plan for your life."[204] Most clients found this hard to deal with but once they accepted the fact that God is in control and if they allowed His Will to be done, their lives would become much more bearable. In Eat this Book, Mr. Peterson states that when one is determined to surrender to God, "things happen because each Scripture begins with the words 'God said.'"[205]

In the book of Job, David Jeremiah points out the conversation that Job had with his friend Bildad. Bildad tells Job that "dominion and awe belong to God."[206] Even though Job was suffering greatly, he held on to his belief that God would make things right again and he was rewarded more than what he previously had.

---

[204] Lawrence Powell. *It's Your Call*. (Tulsa, OK: Victory), 52.

[205] Eugene Peterson, *Eat This Book*. (Grand Rapids, MI: William B. Erdmans Publishing Co, 2006), 60.

[206] David Jeremiah Tried, *Tested and Triumphant: The Book of Job. Vol. 2* (San Diego: Self-Published, 2010), 45.

Clients at CHMCLACC are taught that even though they may think they know what their lives are all about, "there is more to your story than what you have read; more to your song then what you have sung."[207] Clients are reminded that God is not finished with them yet. They must be open to receive the blessings that God has bestowed upon them and to use the gifts that He has given them to better their lives.

Lucado goes on to say in Out Live Your Life, that "God never sends you where He hasn't been."[208]

Accept Christ's Invitation
"Come unto me, ay that labour and are heavy laden, and I will give you rest." Matthew 11:28

How many times have we heard a person say "I don't need any help," or "I can do this all by myself?" The answer to this question is many. But we instruct our counselees that God wants them to come to him. He wants His children to know that all they have to do is come to him and He will answer their prayers. One need not feel inadequate or unworthy because they have fallen short. This is an important time to go to God. He hears their cries and according to His word, He will never forsake them.

---

[207] Max Lucado *When God Whispers Your Name* (Dallas, TX: Word Publishing, 1994), 200.

[208] ____. *Out Live Your Life* (Nashville, TN: Thomas Nelson Publishing, 2010), 138.

"When we rest in Christ, with total honesty, we give him a chance to prove to us that he loves us amidst all our sin."[209] How many times has a person thought that God was angry with him because of something he's done? If this were the case, God would be an angry God. But the God we serve is a loving, caring God. He loves His children, even when they act as if they do not love Him. "If you allow it to happen, relationships with God satisfies all conditions when we seek him."[210] His love for us will never cease. God "issues invitations by the millions"[211] according to Max Lucado. All a person has to do is accept it.

"Our moods may shift, but God's doesn't, our minds may change, but God's doesn't."[212] Mr. Lucado points out a very important aspect in this quote. How many times has a person said "I'm going to do this," or "I'm going to do that," and then change their minds because the process of what he may be going through seem to be too hard. But God never changes. He has remained the same from the very beginning and will remain the same until the very end. All a person has to do is believe and trust in Him.

---

[209] Gregory Boyd. *Seeing is Believing: Experience Jesus Through Imaginative Prayer*. (Grand Rapids, MI: Baker Books, 2004), 107.

[210] Tim Clinton, Gary Sibcy *Why You Do the Things You Do: The Secret to Healthy Relationships* (Nashville, TN: Thomas Nelson Publishers, 2006), 129.

[211] Max Lucado, *3:16: The Numbers of Hope* (Nashville, TN: Thomas Nelson Inc, 2007). 93.

[212] _____. *Traveling Light*. (USA: W Publishing, 2001), 144.

"God is sending signs to everyone, He wants us all to be part of His family."[213] We need to realize that when one refuses God's invitation to come to Him, they can never truly experience His grace and mercy. "God's word is designed to help us, direct us and encourage us in our everyday life."[214] All a person has to do is simply read the Bible. God's words have been an encouraging factor in life for thousands of years. All one has to do is study them and do their best to live by them. There are many stories in the Bible that a person can go to and see similarities in what they may be experiencing. Staying in the word will help to overcome and understand the works of God and prepare a person to combat the bad and replace with the good. What people must realize is God wants all of His children to come to Him, in good times and in bad. He doesn't want His children to use Him as a last resort. This happens a great deal of time. Many people will wait until they are rock bottom or at the lowest point in their lives before they make the decision to take their burdens to Christ.

---

[213] Joan Wester Anderson. *Power of Miracles: Stories of God in the Everyday.* (New York: Ballantine. 1998), 234.

[214] Joyce Meyer. *Power of Simple Prayer: How to Talk with God About Everything.* (NY: FaithWords, 2007), 178.

According to Dr. Towns, "when God invites us into His presence, and, He goes one step farther – He takes us into His very heart." God wants His children in His presence and especially when they are hurt. He brings them to His heart to show them His greatness and how He can guide them on the right path. Bishop Jakes states that "when God wants to accomplish something, whether big or small, he uses ordinary people."[215]

George Barna in *The Power of Vision* points out that God is "personally involved and has created a customized vision for you and you alone."[216] This statement will help one to realize that they are unique individuals. Part of what is done at CHMCLACC is helping clients to identify themselves through temperament studies and self-inventory. Once a person can understand how their minds work, it gives them a better understanding of how to react in certain situations. Mr. Barna goes on to say "We are to love God through full appreciation of who He is and what He has done by allowing ourselves to be spiritually dependent in our lives but we must learn to depend on Him and not man. Man has a way of breaking promises, etc. but God's promises are forever.

.

---

[215] T.D. Jakes *Mama Made the Difference* (NY: Penguin, 2004), 12.

[216] George Barna. *The Power of Vision: Discover and Apply God's Vision for Your Ministry.* (Ventura, CA: Regal Books, 1992), 91.

BIBLIOGRAPHY

Adamson. Marilyn. "Does God Answer Our Prayers?"

http://www.everystudent.com/wires/prayAlcoholics Anonymous. *Alcoholics Anonymous: Big Book 4th Edition.* New York: Alcoholics Anonymous, 2001.

Alford, Henry. *How to Live: A Search for Wisdom from Old People (While They Are Still on This Earth).* New York, NY: Hatchette Book Group, 2009.

All About Prayer. "Healing-Prayers." http://www.allaboutprayer.org/healing-prayers.htm. (accessed 22 January 2010).

Anderson, Joan Wester. *The Power of Miracles: Stories of God in the Everyday.* NewYork: Ballantine, 1998.

Arkwriter. "Prayer Changes Things." http://hubpages.com/hub/prayerchangesthings (accessed 14 November 2009).

Arno, Phyllis J., Richard G. Arno. *Creation Therapy: A Biblical Based Model for Chrisitan Counselors.* 1993.

Arno, Phyllis J., The Messenger, A Bi-monthly Publication: of NCCA, Jan, Feb, 2009 Vol. 66

Atkinson, Brent. "The Emotional Imperative (excerpts). http://www.dearpeggy.com/2-affairs/com022.html (accessed 6 March 2010).

Baker, Dan. Ph.D., Cathy Greenberg with Ina Yalof. *What Happy Women Know – How New Findings in Positive Psychology Can Change Women's Lives for the Better.* NY, Rodale. 2007.

Barna, George. *The Power of Vision: Discover and Apply God's Vision for Your Ministry.* Ventura, CA. Regal Books, 1992.

____. *Think Like Jesus.* Brentwood, TN. Integrity Publishing, 2003.

Basco, Monica Ramiraz. *The Procrastinator's Guide to Getting Things Done*. New York: The Guilford Press, 2010

BenShea, Noah. A Compass for Healing: Finding Your Way from Emotional Pain to Peace. Deerfield Beach, FL. Health Communications Inc. 2006

Blackaby, Henry. *Created to be God's Friend*. Nashville, TN. Thomas Nelson Publishers, 1999.

Bonem, Mike, and Roger Patterson. *Leading from the Second Chair*. San Francisco: Jossey-Bass, 2005.

Borysenko, Joan Ph.D. *Minding the Body, Mending the Mind*. NY. Bantam Books, 1987.

____. *It's Not the End of the World: Developing Resilience in Times of Change*. Australia: Hay House, 2009.

Boyd, Gregory A. *Seeing is Believing: Experience Jesus Through Imaginative Prayer*. Grand Rapids, MI. Baker Books, 2004.

Butler, Gillian, Tony Hope, *Managing Your Mind. The Mental Fitness Guide;* New York, NY: Oxford University Press, 2007.

Bryant, Jamal-Harrison. *World War Me*. Baltimore: Empowerment, 2009.

Bynum, Juanita. *No More Sheets*. Lanham, MD. Pneuma Life Publishing, 1998.

Carbonell, Mels. *How to Solve the People Puzzle: Understanding Personality Patterns*. Blue Ridge, GA. Uniquely You Resources, 2008.

Carducci, Bernardo J., Susan K. Golant. *Shyness: A Bold New Approach: The Latest Scientific Findings Plus Practical Steps for Finding Your Comfort Zone*. New York: Harper Collins Publishers, 1999.

Caringinfor.org.CaringForSomeone/TheTruthAboutPain/PainCareBillofRights.htm.Internet.www.caringinfo.org (accessed 26 December 2006).

Carlson, Richard. *Easier Than You Think Because Life Doesn't Have to be So Hard.* New York: HarperCollins, 2005.

Carson, Ben w/Gregg Lewis. *The Big Picture.* Grand Rapids, MI. Zondervan Publishing House, 1999.

Cheydleur, John R. *Called to Counsel.* Wheaton, IL. Tyndale House Publishers Inc, 1999.

Clark, Lynn. *SOS Help For Emotions: Managing Anxiety, Anger and Depression.* Bowling Green, KY. SOS Programs and Parent Press, 2002.

Clinton, Tim, Sibcy, Gary. *Why You Do the Thing You Do: The Secret to Healthy Relationships.* Nashville, TN. Thomas Nelson Publishers, 2006.

Coleman, Joshua Ph.D. *When Parents Hurt: Compassionate Strategies When You and Your Grown Child Don't Get Along.* New York: Harper Collins Publishers, 2007.

Crabb, Larry. *Connecting: Healing for Ourselves and Our Relationships.* Nashville: W Publishing Group, 1997.

Dale, Robert D., *To Dream Again: How to Help Your Church Come Alive.* Eugene, OR. Wipf & Stock Publishers, 1981.

Davis, Sampson, George Jenkins, and Rameck Hunt. *The Bond.* New York: Penguin, 2007.

Deep, Samuel, and Lyle Sussman. *Yes You Can!* Reading, MA: Addison-Wesley, 1997.

Dimitrius, Jo-Ellen, Mark Mazzarlla. *Reading People: How to Understand People and Predict Their Behavior Anytime, Any Place.* New York: Random House, 1998.

DuBrin, Andrew Ph.D. *Getting it Done: The Transforming Power of Self-Discipline.* NJ. Peterson's/Pacesetter Books, 1995.

Dunson, Donald. *Child, Victim, Soldier: The Loss of Innocence in Uganda.* Maryknoll, NY: Orbis, 2008.

Duplantis, Jesse. *The Everyday Visionary – Focus Your Thoughts, Change Your Life.* New York. Simon & Schuster, 2008.

Dyer, Wayne W. *Your Sacred Self: Making the Decision to Be Free.* New York. Harper Collins Publishers, 1995.

____. *Excuses Begone! How to Change Lifelong, Self-Defeating Thinking Habits.* New York: Hay House Inc., 2009.

Edwards, David M. *Worship 365: The Power of a Worshiping Life.* Nashville, TN. Broadman & Holman Publishers. 2006.

Ehow.com/how 4425346 *deal-emotions*.html (accessed 17 February 2010).

Encyclopedia Britannica. *Encyclopedia Britannica Online.* Encyclopædia Britannica, 2011. http://www.britannica.com/EBchecked/topic/438450/pain (accessed 01 May 2011).

Enright. Robert D. *Forgiveness is a Choice. A Step-by-Step Process for Resolving Anger and Restoring Hope.* (Washington D.C.: APA Life Tools, 2001).

Evans, David G. *Dare to Be A Man.* New York: Penguin, 2009.

Farber, Daniel A. *Retained by the People, the "Silent" Ninth Amendment and the Constitutional Rights Americans Didn't Know They Have.* New York. Basic Books, 2007.

Foster, Mike, Jud Wilhite. *Deadly Viper: Character Assassins.* Michigan: Zondervan, 2007

Frederickson, Barbara Ph.D. *Positivity*. New York. Crown Publishers, 2009.

Gaia.com/quotes/osho_1.Internet,www.gaia.com/qoutes/osho_1 (accessed 26 December 2009).

Gardner, Chris. *Start Where You Are: Life Lessons in Getting from Where You Are to Where You Want to Be*. New York: HarperCollins, 2009.

Gallozzi, Chuck. "Overcoming Adversity." http://www.personal_development.com/chuck/adversity.htm (accessed 12 December 2009).

Gottman, John M., and Nan Silver. *The Seven Principles for Making Marriage Work*. New York: Three Rivers, 1999.

_____. Why Marriages Succeed or Fail….And How You Can Make Yours Last. New York. Simon & Schuster, 1994.

Grant,Mark."OvercomingPain." http://www.overcomingpain.com (accessed 8 March 2010).

Greenspan, Miriam. *Healing through the Dark Emotions*. Boston: Shambhala, 2003.

Harder, Arlene, MA. MFT. "Understanding Pain is the First Step in Controlling It." http://www.support4change.come/health/participate/pain/understand.html. (accessed 18 December 2009).

Healthzine.org. "Pain-Treatment/emotional-pain." http://www.healthzine.org/Pain-treatment/emotional-pain. (accessed 24 February 2010).

Hilliard, I.V. *Secret for a Better Life, Simple Strategies to Improve the Quality of Your Life Today*. Houston, TX. New Spectrum Media Concept, 2007.

Holy Bible, (KJV, NKJV)

Houdmann, M., P. Matthews, and R. Niles. "Healing Prayers: Can I Receive Healing from God If My Faith Is Strong Enough?" http://www.allaboutprayer.org/healing-prayers.htm (accessed 22 January 2010).

Hub Pages. *Dealing With Your Emotional Pain.* http://hubpages.com/hub/Dealing-With-Your-Emotional-Pain.html (accessed 29 January 2010).

Ilardi, Stephen Ph.D. *The Depression Cure – the 6-Step Program to Beat Depression without Drugs.* Cambridge, MA. Da Capo Press, 2009.

Jakes, T. D. *Reposition Yourself.* New York: Atria, 2007.

– – –. *Can You Stand to be Blessed?* Shippensburg, PA: Treasure House, 1994.

– – –. *Making Great Decisions.* New York: Atria, 2008.

– – –. *Mama Made the Difference.* New York: Penguin, 2006.

_____. *He-Motions: Even Strong Men Struggle* New York: Penguin Group, 2004.

_____. *Power for Living.* Shippenburg, PA. Destiny Image Publisher, 1995.

_____. *It's Time to Reveal What God Longs to Heal."* Shippenburg, PA. Destiny Image Publishers, 1995.

_____. *The Great Investment: Faith, Family and Finances.* New York: Putnam's Sons, 2000.

_____. *Maximize the Moment: God's Action Plan for Your Life.* NY: Putnam's Sons, 1999.

_____. *Naked and Not Ashamed: We've Been Afraid to Reveal What God Longs to Heal.* PA: Destiny Image Publishers, 1995.

Jampolsky, Lee Ph.D. *Healing Together- How to Bring Peace into Your Life and the World.* Hoboken, NJ. John Wiley Sons, 2002.

Jeffers, Susan Ph.D. *Embracing Uncertainty – Breakthrough Methods for Achieving Peace of Mind When Facing the Unknown.* New York. St. Martin's Press, 2003.
Jeremiah, David. *Tried, Tested, and Triumphant: The Book of Job.* Vol. 1 & 2. San Diego, CA: Self-published, 2010.
____ . *Living with Confidence in a Chaotic World: What on Earth Should We Do?* TN: Thomas Nelson, 2009.
Karban, Roger. "Becoming a New Person."
http://www.evangelist.org/archive/htm/0213karb.htm (accessed 10 Feburary 2010).
Kashdan, Todd Ph.D., *Curious? Discover the Missing Ingredient to a Fulfilling Life.* New York. William Morrow, 2009.
Keirsey, David. *Please Understand Me II – Temperament, Character, Intelligence*: CA, Prometheus Nemesis Book Company, 1998.
Kelly, Matthew. *A Call to Joy – Living in the Presence of God.* San Francisco. Harpers Collins, 1997.
Kirshenbaum, Mira. *Everything Happens for a Reason.* New York: Harmony, 2004.
LaHaye, Tim. *Spiritual Controlled Temperament.* Illinois. Tyndale House Publishers Inc, 1994.
_____ . *Spiritual Controlled Temperament*, Illinois. Tyndale House Publishers, Inc, 1996.
Lev, Julian, and Zara Kriegstein. *The Meaning of Life: A Child's Book of Existential   Psychology.* Tijeras, NM: Trans-Limbic, 2007.
Lewis, C.L. *The Weight of Glory.* New York, NY. Harper Collins Publishers, 2001.
Lewis, C.S. *Faith.* Nashville, TN. Thomas Nelson Inc, 1998.
_____ . *Mere Christianity.* San Francisco. Harper Collins, 1952.

Lucado, Max. *3:16 The Numbers of Hope*. Nashville, TN. Thomas Nelson Inc., 2007.

_____. *Traveling Light*. W Publishing. USA. 2001.

_____. *When God Whispers Your Name*. Dallas, TX. Word Publishing, 1994.

_____. *Out Live Your Life*. Nashville, TN. Thomas Nelson Publishing, 2012.

Lund, Georgia. "Psalm 6 Bible Study: How To Pray When You Are in Physical or Emotional Pain." http://www.associatedcontent.com/article/1337225/psalms_6_bible_study_how_to_pray_when.html?cat=38 (accessed 9 November 2009).

Martin, Glen, Gary McIntosh. *The Issachar Factor: Understanding Trends that Confront Your Church and Designing a Strategy for Success*. Nashville, TN. Broadman & Holman Publishers, 1993.

Martin, Grant. *Counseling for Family Violence and Abuse*. Nashville: World Publishing, 1987.

Mason, Willie W. *Martin Luther King, Jr. Is the Dream Still Alive?* Bloomington, IN. Author House. 2006.

Mathis, Rick Ph.D. *The Christ Centered Heart – Peaceful Living in Difficult Times*. Liguori, MI. Liguori/Triumph. 1999

Maxwell, John C. *Developing the Leader Within You*. Nashville, TN: Thomas Nelson Inc., 1993.

_____. *Developing the Leader Around You*. Nashville, TN. Thomas Nelson Inc., 1995.

McGowan, Lillian. "You Can Become a New Person." *Passionist,Compassion*,no.52-(Spring1998). http://www.cptryon.org/compassion/spr98/kilian.html (accessed 18 February 2010).

McGraw, Phillip C. *Life Strategies: Doing What Works, Doing What Matters.* New York: Hyperion, 1999.\
———. *Self Matters: Creating Your Life from the Inside Out.* New York: Free Press, 2003.
McKenna, Paul, and Hugh Willbourn. *How To Mend Your Broken Heart.* New York: Three Rivers, 2003.
Merriam-Webster Dictionary. http://www.merriam-webster.com
Meyer, Joyce. *Managing Your Emotions Instead of Your Emotions Managing You.* New York. Warner Book, 1997.
_____. *Power of Simple Prayer: How to Talk with God About Everything.* New York. FaithWords, 2007.
_____. *Battlefield of the Mind.* New York. Faith Words, 1995.
_____. *Eat the Cookie, Buy the Shoes.* New York. Faith Words, 2010.
Mouser. Regina. "Weathering Emotional Storms: Releasing Past Pain." http://healing.about.com/od/mentalemotional/a/emotionalstorms.htm (accessed 28 February 2010).
Munroe, Myles. *Kingdom Principles: Preparing for Kingdom Experience and Expansion.* PA: Destiny Image Publishers, 2006.
Najemy. Robert E. "Dealing With Emotional Pain." http://www.enhancedhealing.com/articles/view.php?article=561&pg=1 (accessed 22 January 2010)
Neeld, Elizabeth Harper, Ph.D. *Tough Transitions: Navigating Your Way Through Difficult Times.* New York. Warner Books, 2005.
North, J. *Wrongdoing and Forgiveness.* Philosophy 62:499-508 Madison, NV: University of Wisconsin Press. Madison, 1987

O'Connor, Richard Ph.D. *Happy at Last – The Thinking Person's Guide to Finding Joy.* New York. St. Martin's Press, 2008.

Orloff, Judith, *Emotional Freedom. Liberate Yourself from Negative Emotions and Transform Your Life:* NY: Harmony books, 2009.

Ortberg, John. *The Life You've Always Wanted.* Grand Rapids, MI: Zondervan, 2002.

Osteen, Joel. *Your Best Life Now.* New York. Warner Faith, 2004.

Osteen, Dodie. *Choosing Life, One Day at a Time.* New York: Free Press, 2006.

Osteen, Victoria. *Love Your Life, Living Happy, Healthy & Whole.* New York. Free Press, 2008.

**Pain.com. "Emotional Pain" www.pain.com/go/default/consumer/emotional-pain/. (accessed 26 December 2009).

Peck, M. Scott. *Further Along the Road Less Traveled: The Unending Journey Toward Spiritual Growth.* New York: Touchstone, 1993.

Peterson, Eugene H. *Eat This Book.* Grand Rapids, MI. William B. EErdmans Publishing Co, 2006.

Petersen, Jim. *Church Without Walls.* Colorado Springs, CO. NavPress, 1992.

Pehrson, Marnie. "Dealing With Emotional Pain." http://marniep.typepad.com/gratitude/2009/06/dealing-with-emotional-pain.html; (accessed 3 December 2009).

Phillips, Bob. *Controlling Your Emotions Before They Control You*: Eugene, OR: Harvest House Publishers, 1995.

Pinds.com. "How to Deal with Negative Emotions." http://www.pinds.com/2007/how-to-deal-with-negative-emotions/ (accessed 11 February 2010).

Piper, John. *Let the Nations Be Glad! The Supremacy of God in Missions*. Grand Rapids, MI. Baker Academic, 1993.

Powell, Lawrence. *It's Your Call*. Tulsa, OK: Victory, 2008.

Rainer, Thom S. The Book of Church Growth: History, Theology and Principles. Nashville, TN. B&H Publishing Group, 1993.

Roberts, Vaughan. *True Worship*. Waynesboro, GA. Authentic Lifestyle, 2002.

Robinson, Marilynne. *Housekeeping*. New York. Bantam Books, 1982.

Rumi. Mevlana J. *"Stream of Consciousness: A Quote on Love and Pain."* www.gaia.com/quotes/osho_1 (accessed 26 December 2009).

Saltz, Gail. *Becoming Real: Defeating the Stories We Tell That Hold Us Back*. New York: Riverhead, 2004.

Schlessinger, Laura. *Surviving a Shark Attack [On Land]: Overcoming Betrayals and Dealing with Revenge*. NY. Harper Collins Publishers, 2011.

Schuller, Robert w/William Kruidenier. *Leaning into God when Life is Pushing You Away*. New York. Faithwords, 2009.

Scriven, Joseph. "What a Friend We Have in Jesus." http://library.timelesstruths.org/music/What_a_Friend_We_Have_in_Jesus/; (accessed 17 December 2009).

Segal, Jeane, and Melinda Smith. "Emotions Communicate! The Powerful Role Emotions Play in All Relationships." http://www.helpguide.org/mental/eq4_emotion_communicates.htm; (accessed 22 January 2010).

Segu, Emmanuel. "Build Your Self-confidence If You Want to Do Well in Life." http://www.selfhelpcollective.com/self-confidence-tips.html (accessed 17 January 2010).

Shahar, Tal Ben: *The Pursuit of Perfect: How to Stop Chasing Perfection and Start Living a Richer, Happier Life.* New York: McGraw:Hill Books, 2009.

Skinner, B.F. *About Behaviorism.* NY: Alfred A. Knopf, 1974.

Schmookler, Andrew Bard. *Out of Weakness – Healing the Wounds That Drive Us to War.* NY: Bantam Books, 1998.

Stanley, Charles. *Living Close to God.* New York. Inspirational Press, 1999.

Summerfield, Frank. *How To Turn Your Prison Into Your Prosperity.* Charleston, SC: Armour of Light, 2005.

Summerfield, Frank, and JoeNell Summerfield. *Singles Prepare! Before You Say You Do!* Charleston, SC: Armour of Light, 2009.

Swenson, Richard A. *Margin: Restoring Emotional, Physical, and Time Reserve to Overloaded Lives.* Colorado Springs: NavPress, 2004.

Towns, Elmer L. *How To Pray: When You Don't Know What To Say.* Ventura, CA: Regal, 2006.

Towns, Elmer L. *Praying the Proverbs Including Ecclesiastes and the Song Of Solomon.* Shippensburg, PA: Destiny Image, 2006.

Towns, Elmer, L., Ed Stetzer. *Perimeters of Light: Biblical Boundaries for the Emerging Church*. Chicago. Moody Publishers, 2004.

Tozer, A.W. *The Knowledge of the Holy: The Attitudes of God: There Meaning in the Christian Life*. New York: Harper San Francisco, 1992.

Tutu, Desmond. *God Has a Dream: A Vision of Hope for Our Time*. New York. Doubleday: 2004.

Vanzant, Iyanla. Peace from *Broken Pieces – How to Get Through What You're Going Through*. New York. Simley Books, 2010.

Viorst, Judith. *Necessary Losses: The Loves, Illusions, Dependencies and Impossible Expectations That All of Us Have to Give Up in Order to Grow*. New York: The Free Press, 2002.

W., Lisa, H. "Dealing With Emotional Pain 92." http://hubpages.com/hub/Dealing-With-Your-Emotional-Pain (accessed 29 January 2010).

Warren, Rick. *Purpose Driven Life*. Grand Rapids, MI. Zondervan, 2002.

_____. *God's Power to Change Your Life*. Grand Rapids, MI. Zondervan, 1990.

Whaley, Vernon M. *Called To Worship*. Nashville: Thomas Nelson, 2009.

_____. *The Dynamics of Corporate Worship*, 2nd Ed. Virginia Beach, VA. Academx Publishing Services, Inc., 2009.

Windale, Rose. "Letting Go of Emotional Pain." **http://www.healthzine.org/Pain** treatment/emotional-pain (accessed 24 February 2010).

Wurmbrand, Richard. *Tortured for Christ*. Bardesville, OK. Living Sacrifice Book Company, 1967

Choosing Hope Ministries
Christian Legal Aid & Clinical Counseling Center
9035 Baltimore Street
Savage, MD 20763
240-294-6324/1-855-382-4668
chmclacc@gmail.com/firstlaw1@gmail.com
Pre-Order Form:

"Getting to the Other Side of Emotional Pain"
By
Rev. Dr. Ronnie Moore, Esq.

Name:_____

Address:_____

City/State:_____

Zip Code:_____

Number of Copies: _____

Price Per Book: $21.99

Total Cost: _____

Please autograph book to_____

www.ingramcontent.com/pod-product-compliance
Lightning Source LLC
Chambersburg PA
CBHW050556170426
43201CB00011B/1717